D0728304

Marriage

DR. RAY GUARENDI

marriage

SMALL STEPS,
BIG REWARDS

franciscan
media
Cincinnati, Ohio

· · ·

Dedication

· · ·

To my wife, Randi (who else?), who makes me
a better husband just by being the wife she is.

· ·

Scripture passages have been taken from *New Revised Standard Version Bible,* copyright ©1989 by the Division of Christian Education of the National Council of the Churches of Christ in the U.S.A., and used by permission. All rights reserved.

Cover and book design by Mark Sullivan
Cover image © Yuri Arcurs | dreamstime

Library of Congress Cataloging-in-Publication Data
Guarendi, Raymond.
Marriage : small steps, big rewards / Ray Guarendi.
        p. cm.
Includes bibliographical references.
ISBN 978-0-86716-985-0 (alk. paper)
        1. Marriage. I. Title.
            HQ503.G84 2011
            646.7'8—dc22

                                        2011002000

ISBN 978-0-86716-985-0

Copyright ©2011, Ray Guarendi. All rights reserved.

Published by Franciscan Media
28 W. Liberty St.
Cincinnati, OH 45202
www.FranciscanMedia.org

Printed in the United States of America.
Printed on acid-free paper.

18 19 20 21 22 5 4

C ONTENTS

A C K N O W L E D G M E N T S

To Cindy Cavnar, my editor at Servant Books, my mental fitness trainer, who has pulled several books from me through healthy prodding, skillful supervision, and well-timed encouragement.

To Leah Bryant, last of a breed, who actually is willing to type my handwritten, legal pad manuscripts. She reads my scrawl better than I do.

To all my clients in marriage counseling over the years. I hope you learned from me. I know I learned from you.

Over decades of working with families, I've learned that I cannot always understand kids and their parents without understanding spouses. In other words, sometimes good parent counseling needs to start with good marriage counseling.

I have also learned that counseling will often end up in a different place from where it started. The discoveries of each session can shift the overall focus dramatically. Not only can the client be surprised by a new direction; sometimes the therapist must totally reassess things too. Or put another way, what we all thought the trouble was may not really be what the trouble is.

My specialty is families. People call me to talk about parenting and discipline: A sixteen-year-old is spiraling out of control, a thirteen-year-old argues with every other breath, a ten-year-old "just won't listen," a seven-year-old has single-handedly launched his teacher into retirement, a four-year-old throws fiery fits that can set off the sprinkler system—in another building.

So while my counseling most often begins with a look at what is going on with a parent or child, it doesn't always stay there. Whatever the initial complaint—a frustrating child, a frustrated parent, a poor discipline style—it often quickly becomes apparent that the core issue is not in the parenting; it is in the marriage. The core issue lies not in how a certain big person gets along with a certain littler person; it lies in how the two big people get along. Parenting struggles may be one sign of marital struggles. The husband-wife relationship can reveal a lot of dissatisfaction unrelated to the original kid-centered upheaval.

The "presenting problem," as we call it in the counseling business, may be young Jacob's addiction to computer games and his resultant crashing grades. Within two visits though, Dad admits to buying all the games because he doesn't see anything wrong with them and to disagreeing with Mom's whole approach to discipline. Further, he considers her too controlling, not only of all things electronic but also of their other two children and of him. As it turns out, his computer game stance reflects an emotional alliance with his son that has formed gradually over the years, while his relationship with his wife has progressively deteriorated.

What might have seemed to be a good commonsense suggestion early in therapy—limit or eliminate the games—becomes unworkable in the face of the conflicted marriage. Dad's resistance will sabotage the most basic of parenting ideas. The course of good family therapy must now involve improving the marriage.

Choosing the Right Focus

Routinely a parent will enter my office with a myriad of complaints about his or her child: Katy talks back, can out-argue a trial lawyer, challenges any and all caretakers, can erupt with the slightest emotional bump, and is the sole reason her nine-year-old brother wants to move out. The situation has been years in developing; now it appears to be an overwhelming and intricate mosaic of discipline bewilderment: "Where do we even begin? And how?" lament Mom and Dad.

Fortunately, although family life may look pretty deteriorated, it can quickly start to improve with some simple ideas. For example, if Katy is a young child, I might advise her parents to send her to the corner for a time at the first gesture of uncooperativeness or defiance. If she's older I might tell them to require a several-hundred-word essay for each and any form of disrespect. And naturally there will be no privileges until the discipline is quietly served.

Nothing too fancy. Just a few initial discipline adjustments. How could such elementary ideas improve matters, especially given the seeming complexities of the discipline brew?

In fact, frequently they do. At the very next session, not uncommonly a parent will express shock at the noticeable change for the better in conduct and attitude, even in "really stubborn" situations. Sometimes trouble spots that have not even been directly targeted, such as sibling quibbling or homework hassles, will respond to one modification. How does this happen? How do such minor adjustments lead to major improvements?

I call it the "cascade effect." The changes, however narrowly targeted, set in motion a whole new positive chain reaction. Now the parent relies on "the corner" instead of arguing or yelling to get cooperation. Katy learns that Mom and Dad mean what they say; thus she argues less. With less arguing, good will has the chance to thrive. More good will elicits more compliments from parents. Katy feels better overall, and she tries harder to please her parents. Mom and Dad feel softer toward this once highly exasperating youngster, and so, while firmer, they become kinder in their approach. As a result Katy spends less time in the corner and more time free from discipline. Everyone's mood brightens as daily agitation declines.

Granted, it takes time to expand such changes into a permanent way of home life, but in the meantime, the family's downward momentum has been arrested and reversed. The family's discord, which had seemed to be as intractable as it was ugly, has proven to be unexpectedly responsive to some relatively easy changes. Small changes can bring big effects.

We see another illustration of this in the field of medicine. If you take two aspirin, you can cure a headache along with neck stiffness, visual sensitivity, nausea, and fatigue. If you take antibiotics for your abscessed tooth, you can quickly alleviate a whole cluster of bodily symptoms—fever, joint pain, muscle aches, lethargy, loss of appetite.

Within psychiatry relatively simple interventions can reduce or conquer a litany of physical troubles. For example, take depression, with its blue mood, social apathy, decreased appetite, poor sleep, self-deprecation, and lack of energy. In many cases all of these symptoms respond well to the mere implementation of an exercise regimen.

No "Secret Keys" to a Happy Marriage

Let's draw a parallel to unhappy marriages. Practically speaking, the puzzle often looks unsolvable: Communication is poor, intimacy is lacking, affection is minimal, disagreements are routine, and arguments turn molehills into mountains. How in the world can you begin to unravel this knot of interrelated struggles?

To be sure, some marriages are seriously disturbed. One or more critical threats assault them: major psychiatric disorders, spousal or child abuse, infidelity, alcohol or substance abuse. But overall, most unhappy unions are not marked by such pathologies. They would more accurately be termed the "daily discontented." On the whole the husband and wife are decent people who would like their marriage to work. Once they loved each other much better, and their warmth was more obvious. Their problems have developed over time, as they drifted apart or as life brought more stresses.

In my experience most marriages, no matter how near the point of no return they may seem to be, can not only pull back from the edge but also dramatically heal and grow in intimacy. Is mine a therapeutic exception to the norm? Not at all. You likely know of marriages that were at one time unpleasant, unfulfilling, even close to divorce. And yet now they have come up from the grave and are actually growing more alive each year. A recent survey confirmed this. When couples in troubled marriages stayed together and were asked five years later about their relationship, 86 percent reported that their marriage was much improved.[1]

How do such weak marriages get stronger? Therapy? Medication? Marriage Encounter weekends? Spiritual guidance? Some. But many resolve to make changes on their own. They try to figure out what went wrong, what's still going wrong, and how to remedy what they can.

If you ask them about their success, you won't hear the titles of self-help books, their "secrets" of a happy marriage, or their "proven" paths to marital fulfillment. In other words, you won't hear ideas known only to a select, emotionally privileged few. You won't hear "techniques" gleaned from marriage counselors. You'll hear how two people, and sometimes only one, determined to make small but highly consequential changes in their attitudes and actions toward each other.

The secret of a good marriage, for the most part, is that there are no secrets, only commonsense, time-tested ideas practiced by countless others who have done it well. Most likely you know many of these ideas already. Yet for reasons particular to you and your spouse, you have ignored them or resisted them, at least until you can get some cooperation.

One Small Step After Another

The ideas in this book infuse good marriages. That's why I present them. You will find no psychobabble, no fancy communication strategies, no grand alterations in lifestyle—just some simple ways to break bad habits and replace them with good ones.

One caution: Just because something is simple does not mean that it's easy. How to treat another better is not rocket science; it's more akin to learning multiplication tables so that we can use them in daily life. In family life—both in marriage and in child rearing—most of us know what to do. We just need to do what we know.

In the rest of this book, I will present one "small step" per chapter. Each simple suggestion will be followed by what I term "resistance rationales"—the most common reactions that husbands and wives have to that particular piece of advice and the reasons that they come up with to not follow it. Then, to illustrate the real-life dynamics in a marriage, I have included a scenario for each step, a dialogue between a husband and a wife—and an anonymous therapist. Each chapter concludes with a "last word" about the step under consideration.

My goal is to make it unnecessary for you to make an appointment with me or any other marriage counselor. While each couple's situation is unique, I think any marriage will benefit from the simple application of these small steps.

Say, "I'm Sorry"

"Say you're sorry." So have countless parents instructed countless kids over countless generations. It's one of Mom and Dad's earliest prescriptions for getting along better with others. It means, let the other person know you regret what you did and want to take a first step toward making it right.

Granted, as anyone with children knows, a kid's apology is routinely marked by an unspoken "sort of," or "not really," or "… jerk!" My observations of my own children and others' have convinced me that for the first several years of life, "I'm sorry" is aimed far more often at the floor than toward any offended human. If floors could speak, they'd probably say something like, "I wasn't the one you stepped on."

Nevertheless, long-standing parental wisdom has been that "Sorry" is a good thing to say, even if you don't want to say it. It's good even if it lacks conviction or flows from a superficial level of understanding. Parents know that the reality behind the words will come, if only inch-by-inch, over the course of a childhood.

Such was standard thinking, that is, until some experts counseled us to rethink our thinking, to become more "relationally enlightened." We were warned not to force a child to apologize and advised to question our parents' and grandparents' ways. After all, they were only training their unremorseful charges in the ways their parents trained them. They mistakenly believed that the mere words "I'm sorry" could help heal a verbal wound or a personal assault. They just didn't realize that "I'm sorry" is a very psychologically complicated offering.

What's more, the experts taught us that without a proper sense of inner remorse, without an understanding of the effect of our conduct on another, indeed, without fully embracing the meaning of the words "I'm sorry," an apology is just, well, words.

That's what the sophisticated, up-to-date theorists say. I'm sorry, but I think they owe us an apology.

Regularly I ask couples, "When was the last time either of you apologized to the other?" Answers vary: "On our first date." "Sometime before our twenty-five-year-old son was born." "Around the time Halley's Comet went by."

You don't have to be a shrink to deduce that apologies are about as welcome a part of their relationship as a tax audit. More often than not, it wasn't always so. They did talk more nicely to each other once upon a time (and Halley's Comet does shoot by once every seventy-six years). Gradually, though, one or both spouses abandoned the practice and any desire to return to it. Thus the feelings wrapped around a good, honest "I'm sorry" died. No feelings, no words.

Our very first small step then to a better marriage is "Say, 'I'm sorry.'" With or without feeling. Don't mumble. Speak clearly. Don't look at the floor. Look at your spouse.

Nevertheless, just as littler humans recoil viscerally from making apologies, so do we bigger humans. Children at least have a valid excuse. They are at the very beginning of their socialization.

They don't yet grasp the value behind the words *I'm sorry*. Their resistance is basic: "I don't want to say that, period. I can tell I don't like the sound of it."

We grown-ups don't like the sound of it either. No matter how much we might know it's warranted and deserved, saying those words means we need to leap an emotional hurdle. Like children, we resist viscerally. We do have our reasons, and to our way of thinking, they're good ones. To quote a psychologist friend, "Anything can be a justification for not doing something you really don't want to do."

Let's analyze and dispel some of our common justifications for keeping our mouths shut when opening them would do some good.

Resistance Rationale #1: "I don't think I have anything to apologize for. I didn't do anything wrong."

Are you Mother Teresa or St. Francis? In nearly all ugly exchanges, it seems safe to say that, if you've not quite reached the apex of spousal sainthood, you did at least a *little* wrong.

The old music group the Monkees admitted in one of their songs to being "a little bit wrong" and allowed the other person to be "a little bit right." It is nice to acknowledge some blame. Most marital "I say/You say" arguments and one-upping put-down matches involve both parties, or they wouldn't rise to the level of nastiness that they do.

Let's say that Jerkface—as labeled by an independent panel of a hundred unbiased observers—is judged to be 42 percent blameworthy in a particular instance. Conversely, She-witch, who started it, fueled it, and verbally slammed it shut, carries an objectively determined 49 percent fault portion. (Let's assume that J. and S. can find a way to lay 9 percent of the blame on their kids.) Now, even though J. and S. can both say, "It wasn't *all* my fault," each has something to apologize for.

To put it bluntly, apologize for your part, however little, of the whole mess—even if you were provoked into saying something nasty, even if you were defending yourself, even if you were acting out of hurt, even if your spouse deliberately tried to antagonize you, even if your blame portion is only 5 percent.

The point is not, do I have a reason for how I acted? Quite probably you do. The point is, do I have anything at all to be sorry for? You are apologizing for what you said or did, completely independent of how much you felt justified in saying or doing it. If you wait to apologize until you absolutely believe the whole scenario was more than 50 percent your fault, well, when is Halley's Comet due to orbit earth again?

If you consider this hard to hear, here's something even harder to hear. Most of us—including me, as my wife can confirm—see ourselves as more innocent than we actually are. We consistently regard ourselves as more pleasant and agreeable and easier to get along with than we really are. In therapy one challenge is to nudge a client toward a more objective self-appraisal.

The desire to scrutinize oneself is not natural. We resist peering into a psychological mirror, particularly one that reflects our foibles and failings. Therefore, work toward accepting the possibility, however remote in your eyes, that your percentage of wrongdoing might indeed be higher than you think. Certainly your spouse thinks so. Probably our independent panel of a hundred objective observers would also serve you a bigger piece of the blame pie than you would serve yourself.

Keep this truth somewhere in your awareness. This should ease the stomach acid buildup at the thought of saying "I'm sorry" for your tiny personal share of offense.

Resistance Rationale #2: "My apology will just convince him that he's right and I'm wrong."

Granted, it could be interpreted that way. But to repeat, your goal is not to assess the correct percentages of blame. Your goal is to acknowledge your own role. "I'm sorry I cursed. That was wrong." "I didn't mean to yell like that. I apologize." "You don't deserve that kind of criticism. Please forgive me."

Note the specifics. You're focusing on exactly what you did, whether it was spontaneous or provoked. If your spouse concludes that you're really confessing, "I'm sorry. This whole thing is my fault," he is wrong. You can expect some of that reaction though, in the short term, especially if your clashes have had a history of escalating into contests of who's right and who's wrong, who wins and who loses. It may take a number of apologies over a number of arguments to finally get across that "I'm sorry" means "for what I said or did" and not "because you were right all along—just as you always think you are."

How many marriage partners eventually come to accept that demarcation? Believe it or not, most do. The hurdle is that the apologizer may not persevere over enough time (weeks? months?) to be rewarded with some softening of the apologizee's "I won again!" attitude. It can be tough to bear, even temporarily, a gloating "I win; you lose" reaction. However, if you can soldier on, weathering your early frustration over the misinterpretation of your apology, in time your words will be understood more accurately.

And if they're not? At least your apology will short-circuit the altercation. According to the Bible, "A soft answer turns away wrath" (Proverbs 15:1). Most people—your spouse included— find it hard to stay emotionally charged when somebody's expression of regret or humility keeps pulling their plug. It changes the dynamics of the situation. Then, as a bonus, your spouse might start to focus on the real meaning of the apology and not on the meaning he wants it to have.

Resistance Rationale #3: "My apology won't be accepted. It will just be thrown back at me."

This is quite possible. To your spouse's ears any apology may sound foreign or forced, especially if she last received one during your wedding rehearsal dinner. If your vocabulary has never included the word *sorry*, you could come across as ill at ease and unsure of yourself. The words might seem as out of place to you as to her.

If you've seldom (never?) said, "I'm sorry," what is your motive now? Your real motive, that is. The fewer and farther between your apologies were in the past, the less likely it is that any present ones, however sincere, will be welcomed immediately with open ears.

Reverse the roles. What if you and your spouse are in the middle of the kind of clash that routinely escalates into severely hurt feelings, and abruptly she expresses some bit of remorse? Wouldn't that stun you, throw you off your emotional balance? "Did I just hear what I thought I heard?" "Does she mean it?" "What am I supposed to do now?" "Am I hallucinating?"

In other words, not only can an apology be hard to express; it can be hard for the other person to digest. In the heat of the interchange, it doesn't seem to belong. Motives are difficult to discern. Instead of lessening the tension, an apology can threaten to become yet another point of contention.

Here is where many spouses abandon the effort. "I'm not going to humble myself just to get humbled." Again, as with disciplining a child (and we grown-ups can be very childish sometimes), the key to success lies in repetition. Your first fifty-two "I'm sorrys" may evoke skepticism or downright disbelief. Your second fifty-two could elicit a mixed reaction—some wariness, some appreciation. Your third fifty-two may be embraced and even answered with an apology.

Now, 156 apologies: Is that three years' worth or three weeks' worth?

Resistance Rationale #4: *"Even if I say it, I won't feel it."*
Not only in marriage but in all of life, if a person waited until he or she felt like it to do what is good and right, many good and right things would never get done. In the words of one social commentator, "How do you reach people who hear with their eyes and think with their feelings?" Acting well often means acting directly counter to our strongest desires or inclinations.

Notice that resistance rationale #4 underlies the "new and improved" child-rearing dictum: "Don't make a child apologize. He likely doesn't feel it, so it's not authentic."

Well before the onslaught of so many experts on life, wise philosophers observed, "Form the habit first; the desire will follow." In our "feelings-are-authentic" culture, we've pretty much reversed that wisdom. We've come to accept the notion that our emotions must point the direction before we can genuinely act in that direction. So we don't behave as we should because we don't feel like it—not yet anyway.

But you don't have to be "authentic" to be effective, especially if what you're forcing yourself to do is positive in the main. There is a sturdy relationship between actions and emotions. Even when a particular feeling only accompanies a particular behavior weakly at the outset, repetition of the behavior will strengthen the feeling. Given enough time, the gap between "I do it" and "I feel it" *will* close. Call it emotional weightlifting. Be aware that the practiced self-discipline of apology *does* get easier with more "reps." (That's "repetitions" for you non-lifters.)

No question about it, in the fury of an altercation, the feelings that dominate will be anything but apologetic. On an emotional spectrum, a heartfelt apology and the so-called authentic emotions of the moment will occupy opposite poles. Consequently, to voice the most tentative, "I'm sorry I used that word," might be asking too much. What if your negative emotions become so overwhelming as to paralyze the slightest conciliatory impulse?

On to Plan B: Apologize later, after the emotional surge has subsided. You can do delayed damage control. At the peak of hard and hurt feelings, you may not be able to bring yourself to acknowledge even 1 percent of personal fault in the face of your spouse's 99. No way, no how, not now can you push out those wretched words. OK, make it your intent to hold them in reserve until you're in a quieter emotional state. An, "I'm sorry for…," retains healing power, whether it is expressed three seconds or three days after an offense.

Of course, if it takes three weeks for you to attain a quieter emotional state, you might have to remind your spouse about the context for your present show of humility. With a time lapse you may not *feel*—there's that word again—as if any remorse is necessary. That was then, and both of you have moved on. Why dredge up what seems to have been somewhat forgotten if not forgiven?

Because your aim is to break the pattern of mutual verbal assault, disengagement, reengagement, cool down, counterattack, uneasy truce. And if you still don't feel sorry three weeks later, please just try voicing the words *I'm sorry*. Good words without good feelings are better than no good words until backed by good feelings. Put more simply, saying is better than not saying.

A caution: Sometimes the delayed apology can reignite the flame. When you come forward with your heart in your hand, you're met with some version of, "Oh, *now* you're sorry," or "What good is 'I'm sorry' now? You should have thought about that then."

Don't be deterred. Remember, your main intent is not to convince your spouse of your genuine regret. Your main intent is to express it. Let your words do your talking.

Resistance Rationale #5: "I may not say, 'Sorry,' but I act sorry." The experience is common if not routine. Someone hurts or wrongs you. He realizes it later if not sooner. A sense of regret overcomes him, leading to a desire to compensate, to make up for his sorry-worthy actions. So he shapes his conduct to present an attitude of "I'm sorry." For a little while he is noticeably more pleasant, more affectionate, overall, nicer. It is his way of apologizing without having to say, "I'm sorry." It is his way of admitting, "I was wrong," without the out-loud, public acknowledgment.

For most of us most of the time, talking good behavior is easier than doing good behavior. Sometimes the journey from our lips to our life is long, meeting lots of resistance along the way. Who hasn't regularly said or heard some variant of, "He talks a good game," or, "Don't just talk the talk; walk the walk"? Self-improvement entails getting more consistent at matching our follow through with our mouths.

In the arena of, "Say, 'I'm sorry,'" the relationship between the talk and the walk seems reversed. For many it is easier to act sorry than to say sorry. One might realize that an apology is deserved and should be given, but the small step of saying so is a big leap. It is less challenging or threatening to display remorse in some way rather than to actually have to admit it, verbally, to the offended person, a spouse no less.

What makes saying harder than doing? Not to sound too psychobabbly, but the reason would appear to be connected to one's self-image. If I admit, "I'm sorry; I was wrong," what else am I admitting? Am I saying I'm a loser? A mean person? Hard to get along with? Am I acknowledging I'm as bad as you accuse me of being?

When a lot of personal implication is attached to an apology, the words themselves become too weighty to utter. We don't want to say what the words imply, especially with someone whom we think might already not think the best of us.

Then too, as we've noted, the spoken is open to rejection. It is a clear-cut admission of wrongdoing, occurring at one definite point in time. What if it lands on closed ears or a still-stinging mood? Being more vaguely penitent could seem the more self-protective course. Because actions are more diffuse, they are harder to rebuff. In a word, they are safer.

But even if you conscientiously shape your actions to speak regret, is that a guarantee they will be so understood? Will the other person hear your unspoken apology? Or will she conclude that you are in a better mood only because the trouble has passed, and you're simply trying to move beyond it, letting it fade away with no further comment? Interpreting the meaning of "I'm sorry" conduct is not always easy.

To turn your actions into words, recognize this reality: An apology is a specific expression of regret for what you did. It is particular to the time, place, and offense. It carries little meaning other than that. "I'm sorry," is not intended to say anything more about you than that you acted wrongly, and for that you apologize.

To be complete, an apology includes both the words and actions commensurate with those words. Either can be the first step, and partial expression is better than no expression. Still, the maximum message is sent when one admits fault in both word and deed.

"Sorry" Scenario

Husband: Just one time I'd like to see you back me up in front of your mother. Just once.

Wife: Oh, like I've never defended you, ever. You've got a real short memory.

Husband: If you have, I wasn't around to hear it. Where she's concerned, I'm never right.

Wife: Did you forget already about last Tuesday? She wanted to take the kids to see that movie you didn't want them to see, and I told her I didn't want that, that I agreed with you, that they're too young for that movie?

Therapist: Sometimes you need to look for the "I'm sorry" opening. Other times, as in this case, the moment is forced upon you by an honest acceptance of the facts.

Husband: You're right. I did forget about that.

Therapist: Now for the next, tougher, verbal step.

Husband: I'm sorry. I shouldn't have said, "You *never* support me." That's not true.

Wife: Well, maybe you ought to get your facts straight before you accuse.

Therapist: The apology was not outright rejected but rather deflected. He can ignore the retort or, if he has the self-restraint, he can press on.

Husband: I'm sorry I accused. But I just don't feel supported.

Therapist: Careful, Husband. He is now justifying his reaction and the "you never" statement. He should try leaving out the last comment, which only returns them both to the source of the argument from a different direction. Rewind.

Husband: I'm sorry I accused. I did forget about last Tuesday.

Therapist: He is not admitting that she always supports him in disagreements with her mother. That's another issue. He is basically trying to defuse this particular point of contention. Further, unless the argument regroups and takes another tack, it is now going to be harder for his wife to challenge him, because for the moment at least, he stopped arguing.

Wife: This is a switch. You actually admitted I'm right for a change.

Therapist: Looks as if two of the possible resistance rationales have been packaged in one statement: Apology not accepted; she'll think she's right and I'm wrong.

He apologized more than once. Not at all bad for a first effort. The guy has potential. The critical question is, can he repeat the "sorry" thing when called for in the future?

The Last Word

There is an unexpected bonus to this whole apology idea. Suppose you've done everything in your verbal and nonverbal power to persuade your never-say-sorry spouse to admit to wrong. You've pleaded, argued, accused, provoked, and cajoled endlessly. Nothing has budged, and perhaps you've about given up on ever being the recipient of any kind of contrition, let alone affection. (Maybe that's why you got the puppy.)

A basic law of human nature says, if you want another to act a certain way, try acting that way yourself. To be more specific, if you want a compliment, give one. If you want to be liked, be likeable. If you want to hear an apology, say one.

As you continue to apologize as needed, you may actually lower your spouse's resistance to doing the same. OK, maybe the ratio of yours to his will settle in at about ten to one. Is that better than the ratio is now?

Have you ever persevered through the process of teaching the most basic manners to a little kid? Say "Please," to get it; say, "Thank you," to keep it; say, "Excuse me," to move past somebody, take your turn, or after a burp. The steps are small and straightforward. What is exhausting is the repetition. It can take fifty thousand times over five years of their lives.

Sorry to tell you this, but I think "I'm sorry" might reside under the same reality. The technique itself is quite uncomplicated. The effectiveness lies in the repetition. But this one small step can work miracles.

| *Don't Say It* |

Is "Say 'I'm Sorry'" a big step for you? Want to make it smaller? Take step #2. You never have to apologize for what you didn't say.

If I could rewrite my life, one of the first chapters I'd edit would include those occasions when I spoke from the rawness of emotion—sometimes not meaning it, sometimes half meaning it, sometimes meaning it only to verbally score. I'd put my family, friends, and colleagues into one big paragraph and write, "I take it back." For whatever I won by my words was short-lived, as I lost later, in my regret and remorse or in another's reaction.

I suppose I could try to excuse myself with some version of, "I didn't know what I was saying." But that wouldn't be totally true. Because I was emotional doesn't mean I wasn't in control—perhaps not fully so but still plenty enough to be aware and responsible.

My professional experience confirms that were counselees more apt to restrain heated words, therapy would have fewer matters to resolve. It's universal: We all speak too quickly for our own and others' good. For the moment the heart beats the head, with unwanted repercussions.

A well-known shoe company has seen its sales skyrocket under the slogan "Just Do It." Apparently this injunction resonates with people. It speaks to motivating action through the power of the will. Would the counterpart, "Just Don't Do It," be equally appealing? Or more to the point, "Just Don't Say It"?

Cutting through the psychoanalysis, the repressed dynamics, the search for the authentic self, much of living well boils down to a decision of the will. I will myself to act good and not bad, to speak well and not poorly. I decide.

Small step #2, "Don't Say It," is a decision not to act or, more specifically, not to speak. Delay saying what you feel most pressured to say for a short time—ten to twenty seconds. The compulsion to verbally strike will drop precipitously.

Regrettable words and disturbing emotions follow a straight-line relationship. The closer in time the words are to the peak surge of emotion, the more likely they are to be nasty, hurtful, or retaliatory. If you can will yourself quiet for just a fraction of a minute, the urge to explode will lose steam. Granted, the emotional aftershocks can linger longer—hours, days even—but seldom at the same level of intensity. And if and when you do speak, your words will be more measured, voicing your point more softly. Hard words, no matter how true, are hard for most anyone to accept.

The sports world uses the phrase, "addition by subtraction." It refers to a team's getting stronger by removing a weak player from the lineup. Lessen the impact of the bad, and you automatically improve the whole. It's new math: addition by subtraction.

Standard advice to struggling couples is to make more time for each other: date nights, couch cuddling, morning coffees, love seats at the golf tournament. The rationale is to put back what is missing, add something positive. Certainly, given mutual cooperation, this will augment good will.

My experience, however, reveals an interesting twist on this theme. It isn't so much adding good times as subtracting bad times that promotes more healing. That is, reducing times of disrespect and harsh words does more to repair the relationship than dinner at Luigi's on Tuesday night. Addition by subtraction.

Of course, to suggest, "Control yourself," at the instant of least control may sound akin to admonishing a fit-throwing four-year-old to " just settle down." It might be what he should do, but he's not of a mind to do it, not until his mood passes anyway. Can we assume that the average grown-up has more self-control than the average preschooler? When was the last time you threw yourself on the floor or kicked over blocks? (You don't have to answer that.)

All lifelong self-improvement is predicated on the core assumption that nearly all of us have a capacity—some more, some less—to assert our will over our impulses. If we didn't, we'd live at the ever present whim of our passions. We'd be buffeted by any person or situation that provoked us.

Then too, everyone has his or her own emotional profile. And some emotions and the words trailing them are easier to rein in than others. A whimpering four-year-old told to "settle down" will do so more readily than one at full emotional throttle.

Social anxiety has never been much of a problem for me. Consequently I've not said too many foolish things out of a sense of social unease. On the other hand, monitoring temper—well, let's just say that as a softball player, I've never clashed with an umpire out of *nervousness.*

I've lifted weights since I was a teenager. (Back then we only had rocks.) Longtime lifters not unusually can bench press three hundred plus pounds. Pushing against that amount of gravity is inconceivable to the beginning lifter. He must start at a number that is achievable but still takes effort. Over some years he may reach that vaunted three-hundred-pound plateau. What was once unthinkable becomes doable.

The emotional parallels the physical. Holding back your tongue (it weighs about four ounces) during maximum emotion might be comparable to benching your own weight on your first trip to the gym. But with measured repetition, you can get there.

Make it your goal to conquer first those instances in which you tend to let your mouth loose but with some exertion could control it. Not every intense emotion challenges your self-control to the max; many if not most could be bridled with some exertion. Begin with the emotional weight you can manage, and you could work your way into pushing up some impressive poundage. But you have to want to do it.

When, for any number of reasons, I don't say what I so desperately want to say, almost always later I am relieved I didn't. I avoid the later guilt and the relational fallout. I don't have to apologize, either. (Unless my wife can read my thoughts…which I wouldn't rule out.)

Resistance Rationale #1: "I can't help the way I feel."
A popular form of counseling is called rational emotive therapy. Its core tenet is that our perceptions precede our feelings. What seem to be automatic emotions are in fact driven by thoughts occurring instantly and sometimes unconsciously. Sometimes these thoughts make sense; sometimes they are irrational and self-defeating. Therapy consists of uncovering and challenging those that are fueling distressing emotions.

Picture yourself waiting inside a crowded bus stop shelter. It's raining hard, and gusting wind is blowing cold spray on everyone, as each struggles to huddle as far back in the shelter as bodies permit. While being jostled you feel what seems to be the point of an umbrella poking the back of your heel. It continues, and so does your irritation. If at that moment I were to ask you what is causing your upset, you'd probably answer with something like, "Somebody back there either is playing his idea of a game or is just flat out oblivious to others."

Because the jabbing is relentless, you reach your emotional limit and finally lurch around to confront the umbrella stabber. It is an elderly blind woman trying to use her cane to stay oriented in the mass of people. What happens to your anger? It immediately dissipates. You don't have to choke it back or talk yourself calm. It is gone in a second, likely to be replaced by other feelings: sheepishness, perhaps guilt.

What you thought was the source of your upset—a jab in the foot—was not. The source lay deeper. It was rooted in your perception of who was doing what to you. The instant your perception changed, so too did your feeling.

A common mood-inflamer is personalizing, the inclination to interpret an incident, interchange, or reaction as another's comment on us, a personal attack. Sometimes it is; sometimes it isn't. Yet few perceptions can make us madder more quickly than a perceived assault on the self.

A wife will reveal in counseling that her husband pursues his wants with little thought of her wishes. She sees this as willfully neglectful and demeaning of her womanhood. At the point of peak hurt, she will unleash hurting words of her own.

The husband, on the other hand, says his wife routinely shows the kids twice the affection she's shown him anytime in the past year. He reads her motherly warmth as deliberately positioning him lower in the family, and he will tell her so with a vengeance, right when she's cuddling with a child.

Both are attributing the worst of motives to the other. True, each spouse's conduct may be insensitive, but it may not have the "in your face" component that is judged so infuriating.

Parents routinely ask me, "How can I avoid getting so quickly frustrated with my kids' behavior?" I often answer with a question: "What is going through your mind as the frustration rises?"

Leading contenders are: "This conduct reflects my poor parenting," "He is deliberately acting bad to make me mad," "This is just one more sign that my child will be on *Springer Jr.* someday." Not to deny some accuracy to any of these, as a rule none are so valid as the parent believes. Yet it is these beliefs that are spiking the exasperation that is spiking the words a parent wouldn't typically say to anyone else—except perhaps a spouse. In essence it isn't the kids' behavior so much that provokes us; it's the meaning we attach to that behavior.

When you're feeling the pressure to speak ugly words, ask yourself, "What am I telling myself right now? What thoughts are fueling my emotions?" Tone down the thoughts, and you'll tone down the emotions.

Be your own counselor. At the minimum it could save you some money.

Resistance Rationale #2: "I speak my mind."

The question is, are you speaking your mind or your emotions?

Speaking my mind implies speaking my thinking. This is how I see things, not just right now but consistently. "I wonder whether you even love the kids, given the way you berate them." Is this my durable impression, or is it an accusation sparked by upset?

Strong emotions can distort our sense of reality. So when we speak our minds, we may be speaking as we think things are, not as they really are, or even as our spouse thinks they are. I certainly don't want my wife to enlighten me about what's coursing through her brain at the very instant she's feeling most poorly inclined toward me. I'd prefer to have some of that impulse settle before she translates it into words.

Conversely, suppose at the boiling point of a heated exchange, I blurt out, "Your parents raised a princess who still thinks everybody, including me, should be her subjects." How plausible is that? Will I still think so later when I've settled?

A few decades back a big push from the social sciences was toward self-assertiveness. A slew of popular books (for example, *Looking Out for #1*) captured the zeitgeist of the movement, which asserted that to achieve proper psychological balance, one needed to make his wants known, needs met, thoughts heard, and feelings respected. Too many people, so the theory went, allowed themselves to be relationally stunted and shunted and were advised to grow bolder.

Not many would argue that this philosophy has no merit, but like all psychosocial trends, it is susceptible to excess. Hypervigilant self-assertiveness can come off as pushy obnoxiousness. Speaking out without a proper consideration of another is asking to be shunned. If I'm not careful, I could "assert myself" into social isolation.

Within a marriage too much assertiveness isn't pretty. Too much "mind-speaking" doesn't do anybody much good. As we've said, some of the most hurtful, self-protective urges can roar into the head when one is feeling his wants and needs are being neglected or demeaned. Assertiveness can rapidly morph into nastiness as emotions drive the discourse harder.

That's my opinion. And you'd better accept it.

Resistance Rationale #3: "I have to vent."

The need to vent is an idea long in residence on the psychological landscape. One of its early names was *catharsis*, the outward expression of one's inner state. Engaging in such, supposedly, was good for one's emotional makeup, analogous to purging the debris from the mental attic. Once cleared, emotional rebuilding could commence.

Born in the minds of clinicians, certain notions readily mature into the broader culture. "Nobody has to guess how I feel; I have to get some things off my chest; it's not healthy to stifle your true feelings; it's better to get your feelings out than to develop an ulcer." (As an aside, we now know that ulcers are caused by bacteria, not stress.)

Conventional wisdom dies hard. The more familiar the concept, the longer it takes to diffuse from the popular consciousness if it's wrong. The catharsis theory is a classic example.

Newer studies offer a quite different conclusion from the older theories. Rather than lowering internal distress, a vent tends to raise it. That's right. The belief that pouring out my every feeling, opinion, or disagreement will in the long run make me feel better is at the least debatable and at the most downright false.

Have you ever watched rainwater run off saturated ground? It finds the dirt path of least resistance. It forms its own little roadway, which channels deeper and faster with every rain.

Emotions and any rough words riding with them are like rainwater. The more they flow with abandon, the easier they flow in the future. Put another way, venting can become freer with each vent. It becomes the response of first choice.

This is not to say that stifling swelling emotions is always good and voicing them is always bad. Obviously, the thoughts beneath the feelings ultimately need to be aired and shared. It is to say that discharging damaging words too readily can become an animal too unruly to restrain.

A chaplain in the military told me that, many more times than once, at peak upset he has headed into the cyber sphere to type his immediate complex of reactions to the offending party. He has learned the hard way to let that e-mail sit in his computer until the next morning. Very few leave his outbox. As he's concluded, "'Send' is not your friend."

No psychological stunting follows from the delay of catharsis. First of all, stirred up feelings routinely are transitory. There is little need to vent them. They will subside on their own.

Even more significantly, full airing of feelings now often generates more distressing feelings later: guilt, sadness, regret, self-punishment. None may be worth the illusory gain gotten from "letting it out." The latest research confirms: Not only does venting lead to more venting; it can also lead to feeling worse.

One more downside: Venting freely is risky to one's physical health. Those who regularly exert sound and fury the minute they feel it are more prone to physical troubles. Ulcers may not arise from stress, but a whole host of other ailments do, or are exacerbated by it.

Venting is necessary for bathrooms and clothes dryers. It comes with a cost to people, both to the venter and the ventee.

Resistance Rationale #4: "I feel better afterward."

When afterward? A minute? An hour? A day?

How soon you feel good, or how much you feel bad, could depend upon when you measure it. As this Resistance Rationale is an emotional cousin to the one previous, the answer to it is likewise related.

No question, some sense of eased tension can follow a spasm of words. Like steam fighting its way free of a boiling kettle, pent-up words build to release from the pressure of emotions. What remains to be known, however, is whether any resultant relational fallout or self-inflicted punishment will be worth the momentary gratification.

Life is brimming with temptations that, if surrendered to for temporary pleasure, could have broad and lasting ruinous repercussions. In the words of the baseball movie hero Roy Hobbs, "Some mistakes you never stop paying for." Fortunately those are few in most of our lives. It is true, nevertheless, that you might pay for some mistakes a long time. And misspoken words are the most frequent of mistakes for many of us.

In the midst of a discipline disagreement with my wife, I might think I'm going to score the winning basket by shooting, "You're about as erratic a parent as I've seen." By tomorrow I recognize what a bizarre exaggeration that is. By tomorrow my wife is still stinging badly, as much of her identity is tied to her motherhood, and my attack pierced straight to the core of who she is. If I didn't anticipate this, I'm going to experience it somehow, someway in the next days or longer.

You just can't know how hard a sarcasm, retaliation, or verbal smack is unless you hit another with it and then watch the size and color of the bruise formed. That's very risky to both of you in exchange for a brief sense of release.

Couldn't one argue a parallel to the observation, "After a good cry, I feel better"? True, tears are a pain reliever. In fact, the chemical composition of tears works some stress reduction physiologically. That's pretty much where the analogy ends.

First of all, tears don't assault another. Tears fall on our cheeks. Ugly words fall on another person's ears.

Second, tears can have a draining effect. They create a true catharsis, if you will, by releasing pent-up emotions. Despite what they might feel like, escalating words, as we've noted, have little or no cathartic up side. Instead they have a synergistic effect: They feed upon one another, not only provoking a spouse toward the same but also pressuring the one mouthing them into louder and meaner stuff. Like a feedback loop caused by a microphone too close to its speakers, words can rapidly rise in tone and volume until something explodes. Tears diffuse; words amplify.

The "better" feeling after hasty, nasty words is an illusory feeling. Perhaps there's a bit of emotional release or some satisfaction at retaliating in kind. But the feeling, even if authentic, may not be long lasting. And even if there are few regrets after speaking, the damage done to a relationship can be costly.

Resistance Rationale #5: "I want to shock."

One of television's most popular early programs was a police drama. Routinely one of the lead detectives, after apprehending the bad guy and tiring of his excuses, would close the deal with a one-line verbal slap: "Maybe that's why they call it 'dope.'" Or, "Different stories, same ending." Whereupon the criminal would react with a look of shocked insight, indicating he had been convicted with self-revelation.

Shaking someone with a well-timed, well-worded comment, nasty or otherwise, is a staple of TV scriptwriters. Generations of shows, drama and comedy, have entertained us with the supposition that sometimes people just need to be hammered with an on-target observation about themselves, and self-scrutinizing change can commence.

The idea has merit. After all, we counselors aim for something similar, though without scriptwriters. Throughout the therapeutic dialogue we listen for the opening to offer a brilliant, life-altering perception that can uncover some hidden motive or pull together seemingly disparate threads of thought.

The critical difference between some of TV, most of therapy, and marital exchanges is one of style. Giving someone our version of the hard truth can be done hard or soft. In the middle of a spousal clash, hard can take precedence, not surprisingly, as the points and counterpoints fly. In fact, the words can be well aimed regarding substance; it's the delivery that invalidates them. A shock effect only works if there isn't too much shock.

Picture yourself in the returns line at a department store. The person in front of you is clearly itching to speak his piece. Once facing the clerk, he unleashes a torrent of disgruntlement with the product, the store, the world. Unless given immediate and full satisfaction, he will sue anyone who ever produced, stocked, or even looked at his fraudulent item.

His obnoxiousness aside, how much of what he's saying is legitimate? Who knows? His fury is clouding his point. How much is honest thinking and how much is shock effect is almost impossible to sort out.

Further, while the shock effect is high, the credibility is low. Clearly this person is speaking through heavy emotion, and no doubt, the clerk has heard similar diatribes before. Though courteously responsive, on the inside she doesn't afford him much credence.

Words can stun for many reasons. They are hurtful, they are accusatory, they are personal, they step on a live nerve, they are dead on target. I may intend to shake up my spouse's world, but my meaning, if spoken through a cloud of upset, can be lost. The effect I think I'm creating may not be the one I am creating. Human nature resists accepting anything if it comes in an ugly package.

The relationship is straightforward: The harder the words for another to hear, the softer the tone needed to get them across.

Don't Say It Scenario

Wife: This is at least the sixth time I've asked you to please get your boxes out of the kitchen. I keep tripping over them.

Husband: Six times is less than your usual total.

Therapist: To make a small disagreement sour fast, go with sarcasm. Few things grate like a mocking rejoinder.

Wife: Oh, now it's my fault because I'm a nag. You haven't touched those things, and you promised two days ago.

Husband: Like I haven't done anything around here in the past two days. When you want something done, you want it done in your time. I'd better jump.

Therapist: From a bicker over boxes, this exchange moves almost immediately into, "Oh, yeah, so are you." A law of arguments is at work: The more recurrent the disagreement, the faster the personal critiques escalate.

Wife: You seem to have plenty of time to get done what you want to get done. If it's your thing, it gets attention. If it's mine, whenever you get to it is fast enough.

Therapist: Wife is taking Husband's box behavior personally, as an indication that he cares little about her feelings. It is her sense of being disregarded that is fueling her words.

Husband: You know, you're a lot like your mother. Dave [his friend] always says, "If you want to see what you're going to live with, look at her mother."

Therapist: Owww. A double insult: a personal affront to the wife and a slam on her mother. It is absurd in its generalization and nasty on several levels. Double insults may sound wittily pointed, but they deserve a heavy delay, stuffed down until the urge to strike with them subsides some.

Wife: Dave always gives his opinion on things that don't concern him, and you go along, no matter how ridiculous. I'm not the only one who thinks so. My dad and even the kids have noticed.

Therapist: Are the boxes still in the kitchen?

A standard byproduct of remarks that should go unspoken is retaliation in unkind. *If Husband goes after her mother, she'll go after his best friend. Then, calling in eyewitnesses, she cites her father—particularly effective if Husband admires him—and the kids.*

Pulling others into one's cause—likely against their knowledge—adds no weight to a criticism. If I'm not about to believe it just because you say so, how likely am I to believe it just because you say others say so?

Husband: Let me put my shoes on, and I'll get rid of the boxes right now. Happy?

Therapist: With one last piece of sarcasm, Husband abruptly returns to the original trouble spot—the boxes. Why? It's hard to know. Defeated? Exhausted by the random arguing? Reeling from the "my dad and your kids" remark? Whatever, for now the argument is finished.

But the stings are not. Sarcasm, double insults, citing witnesses—all rank high in the "Don't Say It" pyramid. They don't resolve; they don't persuade; their aftereffects linger long. Likely, parts of this conflict will be resurrected in both spouse's heads on their next visit with Wife's mom and dad.

There is a bright side. These sorts of reciprocal verbal cuts can allow a lot of practice at "I'm sorry."

The Last Word

Talk radio programs employ a "broadcast delay." This is the time between what a caller says on the phone and when it is heard on the air. Standard delay times are anywhere between seven and twenty seconds, providing a technological protection against crude, ugly, or highly inappropriate talk. If a caller engages in such, only he, the host, and the studio staff will hear it. No radio listener will ever know what he said.

"Don't Say It" is a self-imposed broadcast delay. It is a protection against remarks that come into the head and should die there. An externally imposed broadcast delay is 100 percent effective. A self-imposed delay is variously so, depending upon the exertion of the will. Regardless, any percentage of stifled ugly talk brings a return well above the seven to twenty seconds of effort to control it. And the one person who doesn't hear it may be more important to you than the largest of radio audiences.

To paraphrase a veteran comic, it's easy to be kind: Just think of something mean, then, *don't say it.*

| *Listen a Minute* |

Perhaps it's coincidence—or perhaps some farsighted linguist planned it so—but *listen* and *silent* contain the same letters.

Countless books have been written on the art of silence and its cohort, listening. Whole therapies have been wrapped around professional listening. Terms like "active listening" (the good kind) versus "passive listening" (the bad kind) permeate the counseling, and even child-rearing lexicons. Ironically, few subjects, it seems, have been talked about as much as has listening.

Our everyday language likewise is full of pithy sayings about the value of listening: "A closed mouth gathers no foot," "You're hearing, but you're not listening," "God gave you two ears and one mouth because he expects you to do twice as much listening as talking." One more, from an anonymous source:

> His thoughts were slow; his words were few
> And never formed to glisten.
> But he was a joy to all his friends,
> You should have heard him listen.

My intent is not to talk about how, why, when, and where you should give an ear to your spouse. Plenty of how-to instruction manuals are available for that. My aim is to distill your willingness to listen down to one small step that can bring maximum results with minimum effort.

To begin, it's nearly impossible to open your ears if your mouth isn't closed. *Listen* and *silent* are anagram companions, but the relationship is one-directional. You can be silent and not listen; it's really hard to listen and not be silent.

Small step #3 begins with the unspoken, "Shut your mouth." What kind of advice is this? Shut up? If I could do that, you might be thinking, we'd do half the bickering, or the bouts would last one-fourth as long.

Knowing the challenge that stifling our urges and our words can be, my advice is basic. Put a time limit on your silence. How about one week? One day? One hour? OK, how about one minute?

Mr. Spock, from the television series *Star Trek*, had a perfectly honed sense of time. He could gauge one minute to within several decimal points. Also he was part Vulcan and thus genetically rational. If you're not a Vulcan, you may have to estimate one minute, not to mention labor to stay rational. Setting a timer would be a bit provocative, as would staring at your watch or, worse, wielding a stopwatch. Your message wouldn't be, "I'm listening"; it would be, "I'm giving you only so much time."

You could surreptitiously glance at the clock. You could mentally estimate your preferred time frame. You could silently count to sixty, though this might distract you from the priority at hand; then again, it might aid you in staying calm. Can you count to six thousand?

A listening time-out slows any accelerating word spiral. By staying quiet, even temporarily, you shut off your share of the "I say, you say." Your spouse has nothing to connect his comebacks to, because nothing's being said. He may yet wax uninterrupted —one doesn't need cooperation to gain tirade momentum. Still, the chances of a verbal barrage are fewer with no return volleys from you.

Recall a key instruction of a good apology: Don't look at the floor; look at your spouse. This applies well to a sixty-second listen. Look at your spouse. Create the impression that you intend to attend to what she is saying. This means no yawning, no studying the ceiling, no adolescent-like rolling of the eyes, and no staring at the TV—especially if it's off.

Any nonverbal cue that displays disinterest, dismissiveness, or disdain won't just undo the pacifying power of listening; it will provoke the opposite reaction. It will agitate. Your aim is to show interest, not to replace spoken messages of disgust with unspoken ones.

Where do you insert your moment of silence? Two prime places: one, at the outset of a subject that has a history of rapidly going negative; two, as soon as the temperature of any exchange gets noticeably hot. In essence you want to lower the volume before it hurts someone's ears. Whereas an apology is an overt response, silence is covert. It requires no action, no words, no expression of feelings, no, "Let me tell you something."

What if you're not very good at discerning when to stop, look, and listen? That's not unusual. The skill comes with practice. And you'll have plenty of practice if disagreements mark your married life.

Further, in analyzing your disputes you might discover a fairly predictable pattern. Most turn rough at particular junctures or impasses. Give credence to your sense of timing. Your intuition will tell you when the dialogue is on the edge of falling fast.

One more point: You can listen for sixty seconds at any time. Don't be pressured by the thought, "Whew, I'm glad I got that over with early. Now I can speak up before I explode." Some spouses intersperse their silence throughout the noise, using it as a sort of control knob on hot emotions. It all begins with mastering that first minute. The stamina evolves.

Resistance Rationale #1: "I can't stay quiet, much less listen, for one minute."

That's why I didn't suggest ten minutes, or five, or even two. One minute is a natural target. It's a basic measure of time, it's easy to remember, and it really is doable, even if initially it seems like a long shot.

What is the standard caveat for every type of exercise program? Start slowly. That's because no sedentary person at a minute's notice can jump up and run a mile, much less a marathon, or bench press his own weight, much less three hundred pounds.

What impacts nearly all first-time exercisers? The painful revelation of how out of shape they are. Nevertheless, if they train past those initial uphill weeks, they are surprised at their gains. Soreness becomes a memory.

If a one-minute listen is your marathon, listen as long as you can. Don't quit the program because you fail to reach the finish line.

Many people cease exercising soon after starting because they're discouraged at their starting level. The paradox is, had they persevered, they'd have fast left that level behind. A rookie jogger might get winded thinking of running a mile. To a veteran jogger, running a mile is a walk in the park.

So it is with emotional self-discipline. At the beginning everything in you is screaming to take a deep breath and spew, but over time you will be able to take a deep breath and hold back. Your, "I can't stay quiet for even one minute," might become, "I can't even carry on for one minute." (I said "might.")

Resistance Rationale #2: "What I hear could upset me."

Being a good listener is easy. I've discovered the secret. Any time, any place, I can give my wife my rapt attention for hours, provided she lists in alphabetical order all my admirable attributes. She would say she doesn't need hours—only an egg timer.

Most anybody can listen well, given that the feedback is positive. The real test is to listen well to the negative. To borrow from Einstein, time is relative. One hour of praise can seem like one minute. One minute of critique can seem like one hour.

It's natural to worry that silence will invite critique. Without interrupting and defending yourself, are you leaving yourself wide open to a sustained verbal pounding?

First of all, is what you risk hearing a total surprise? Have not your past disagreements routinely revolved around the same themes? Just as kids misbehave in mostly the same ways—disrespect, sibling quibbling, chore shirking, bedtime bad times—so too do spouses wrangle repeatedly over the same topics. Thus, much of what you will hear is nothing you haven't heard before, many times. By itself silence doesn't usually provoke new stuff.

Second, what do you gain by answering immediately? If this has been your history, has it worked? Or has it only led to fodder for more contention and therefore to hearing even more words you don't want to hear? It's safe to say that reacting too quickly to accusations and provocations leads to meaner stuff than does silence.

Third, you're probably not planning to stay quiet indefinitely. Shortly you will answer, likely in less than one minute. Arguments aren't radio contests, in which if you don't call in within the minute, your chance to win has passed. Your spouse's perspective won't become more deeply rooted because you didn't debate it instantly.

Last, and hardest to hear, maybe what you'll hear by your silence is what you need to hear. If I focus on my wife's perspective instead of my next answer, I'll better comprehend her perspective, even if I don't like it or agree with it. Silence invites information, some of which may be needed and good.

Resistance Rationale #3: "My spouse will think I agree."

That could be. If, however, after one minute you begin disagreeing, she'll quickly realize hers was a wrong first impression. Not that I'm suggesting you be anxious to alter that impression. It's just that a disagreement tends to drift toward more disagreement, for a while anyway.

Your listening is simple listening. You're not obliged to "therapeutically" listen, replete with sensitive "Mm hmms," "Yes, I see," "Tell me more," "I hear you saying…". I'm a therapist, and I don't talk like that. You can if you want, and after your spouse gets past her initial suspicion that you secretly enrolled in some online communication course, she may conclude that the new, responsive you is in fact agreeing with her.

In counseling, regularly I listen long, as people tell me all about themselves and their lives. Sometimes I agree with their perceptions and judgments; sometimes I don't, and they'll hear from me soon enough. My sustained silence in no way implies that I think what they're saying is realistic, helpful, or sound. Within a few sessions it can become painfully clear that a lot of thinking will need to be analyzed and adjusted.

Still, at the outset I must listen. Otherwise my guidance could be premature or inaccurate. My ultimate intent is to know better how they approach life, so I can help them better approach life. If they misinterpret my attention as confirmation, I can address that later.

So it is in marriage. You may not listen as long as I do in therapy. That may be because you don't need to. Most likely you understand your spouse better than I understand a client. You've lived with him for years. Nonetheless, in listening a bit more than you formerly did, you may sound a bit more informed when you do speak. Whereupon your spouse will hear that your silence was not necessarily acquiescence.

What if your spouse does think silence is agreement? Is that always a problem? Are there not times when, if you mulled it over, you could find legitimacy in her stance?

My wife, Randi, and I don't always mesh minds on bedtime for the kids. My work schedule can be unpredictable, so occasionally in the evening I will politic for a little more TV time with the younger ones. Randi, on the other hand, is the primary domestic schedule setter. She is the one to bear the brunt of the next day's sleepy, cranky children.

Rather than interrupting her when she announces bedtime and reiterating my reasoning from six angles, if I shut up and listen, I may better understand her side. Not only that, but she may better understand mine if I don't jump in immediately debating with both feet. And as sometimes happens, we negotiate a compromise. (For example, she'll let me pay her for every minute longer the kids can stay up. It is a compromise, as I talk her down to half her original price.)

Resistance Rationale #4: "What if I look and feel dumb?"

I figure it this way: I can stay quiet and risk looking dumb, or I can speak and risk sounding dumb too. In the words of the popular axiom, "It is better to keep your mouth shut and let people think you're foolish than to open it and remove all doubt."

Of course, as a father of ten children, I look dumb a lot. For me the worry is slight that by listening I would look much different from normal.

To be sure, all manner of unspoken words can at any time cross one's face: disdain, apathy, disbelief, bewilderment, shock. Just because you're quiet doesn't mean you're not commenting. The major challenge is not merely to avoid looking dumb; you could do that by looking at your feet. The major challenge is to corral and control any feelings semi-automatic with being provoked. My wife is far less irked by my husbandly "deer in the headlights" daze than by my other faces conveying, "What are you talking about?"

Looking dumb isn't always bad. Sometimes it's a much better option than too quick and too ugly a retort. If you do want to look smarter, look directly into your spouse's face, particularly his eyes. It's hard to study someone's countenance and appear lost.

Perhaps you're really thinking, "Did I leave the iron on?" Still, you do look as if you're engaged. And that could perplex your spouse, possibly make her a bit paranoid, as she wonders, "What are you staring at?"

Listen Scenario

Wife: This is the third time this week you came home over an hour later than you said you would.

Husband: I'm sorry. I should have called.

Therapist: Listening does not preclude any and all words. Sometimes it's good to suspend silence for an apology.

Wife: When you don't call, I feel like I don't matter. You're just pursuing your desires without a thought about how it affects me and the kids.

Husband (looking, listening, as if to say, "Go on.")

Therapist: Wife is surprised by the lack of defense, so she heads in another direction.

Wife: I don't remember the last time you called to tell me you were going to be late. It's a matter of simple courtesy. You do it for any meeting at work or with your friends.

Therapist: Still listening, Husband could now be fighting the urge to retort with something like, "Maybe I don't call because I don't want to get grief twice—once on the phone and once when I get home." Nevertheless, exhibiting self-restraint, he acknowledges.

Husband: I know. You're right.

Therapist: Any kind of agreement counts as listening. It is, in effect, verbal listening.

Wife: You know, I call you when my plans change. I take into consideration your schedule. I don't just do whatever and let you try to figure out where I am or what happened.

Therapist: For Wife to argue when no argument is being returned is getting harder. For Husband to not argue when the accusations are building momentum will get harder. Still, holding his peace a little might be enough to keep any skirmish from getting out of hand.

Wife: Are you going to say anything? Are you just shutting me out?

Therapist: Silence, like an apology, can be misinterpreted, especially when unexpected. Spouses don't naturally conclude, "Golly, he's just trying to be a whole lot more agreeable about all this than he has been the previous 192 disagreements." Rather the first impulse is to think, "This is just a different tactic than I'm used to."

When asked a direct question, it's wise to respond. If not the silence could come across as rudeness or tacit provocation.

Husband: I'm just listening. I'm not trying to shut you out. I'm trying to hear you out.

Therapist: If Husband really wants to earn extra credit, he could say something like, "I'm trying to listen for a change," or, "I really want to understand your point." Then Wife would say,

Wife: Have you been secretly going to counseling? Are you on drugs? Are you an alien being who has taken over my husband's body? What did you do with my husband?

Therapist: All right, maybe she wouldn't, but she could think it. Nonetheless, if one spouse can listen through any initial suspicion or resistance, the other may be shocked into listening back.

The Last Word

A few moments of attentive listening are not relational magic or conversational elixir. Call them more of a balm. The smallest amount of listening can give and beget respect. It says, "I'm taking in what you have to say."

In return you may find that listening is easier on your nerves than responding verbally, tit for tat. Both the listener and the listenee will automatically have less to fight about. Peace will be a reward for your silence. Really. Are you listening to me?

| *Ask a Few Questions* |

Back in graduate school I absorbed a lot of counseling theories and techniques. Fashionable at the time were those that emphasized "reflective listening," that is, mirroring to the client the feelings underlying his words. "So you get frustrated when your wife doesn't understand your perspective," "You feel betrayed when he treats strangers with far more consideration than he treats you."

Central to this mode of communication was the dictum "Curtail the questions." Questions don't really expose the all-important internal state, and they can distract from the main goal: understanding where a person is emotionally "coming from."

Current marriage and family guides also reflect this focus on feelings and the questioning of questions. One popular parenting course, in its section on "how to" communicate with adolescents, strongly advises asking no questions, as questions are a form of interrogation. Really?

Should I ever meet that program's author, I'd have a few questions for him. If one travels outside the bounds of such contemporary views, common sense and experience will teach that honest, probing questions are, and always have been, fundamental to human connection.

Have you ever met someone, chatted a while, and quickly formed a favorable first impression? What was it, you wondered, that made her so appealing? Then you realized. She was genuinely interested in you. She asked about your family, your job, your activities. She wanted to know the bits and pieces of who you are and was much less invested in giving you her story and opinions. Somehow she deftly kept the focus on you, mostly through questions.

I have five sons, three of whom are of dating age. That means they're in their thirties. (Just kidding...sort of.) At about age seventeen my son Jon asked me, "Dad, how do I talk to girls so they're comfortable with me?"

My wife, standing nearby, heroically struggled to hide a look that said, "Let's see if Ray has learned anything at all since we dated."

I advised Jon to ask a young woman about her life—parents, siblings, school, career plans, hobbies. Let her answers guide the conversation elsewhere—likes and dislikes, opinions, church involvement. Don't be driven to talk about yourself. Show her you want to hear about her.

Most likely you know some basics about your spouse: her age, where she works, whom she is married to, the names—including middle—of your kids. If you're a guy, you'd better at least have some good guesses. Not uncommonly, however, I will ask someone how his spouse gauges, say, his level of household help, and he'll reply, "I don't really know for sure."

Do you know how your spouse thinks, particularly in areas where you disagree? What are his reasons for disciplining as he does? Why is he insecure over the time you spend with your best friend? Can you explain her frustration at not getting more cooperation from you and the kids? Why does she maintain that you watch way too much television?

You don't have to concur with her thinking. But can you explain it—somewhat? You likely have heard her frustrations repeatedly. If the why is not all that clear yet, why not? Do you think her reasons are ridiculous? Overreactive? Emotional? Muddled? Are you so itching to retort that you only partially hear her out?

Typically my first few counseling sessions are spent eliciting background. What is the main issue? What are the side issues? What is the history? As in marriage, some people readily offer a detailed picture of their inner selves. Others need to be drawn out. So I begin to inquire, which leads to answers, which then leads me to more questions.

What I hear I may not understand, agree with, or think is good. What I hear may make no sense whatsoever given what I heard six minutes before. Nevertheless, I have to be able to grasp and reiterate a client's reasoning and perceptions. It is critical that I ask enough to get to what I need to know.

Small step #4 is "Ask a Few Questions," or more if you are so inclined. Why? To get more information. Why? To more fully understand. Why? To turn your energies from what you're about to say to what your spouse is already saying.

When upset, who can do this? Maybe the better question is, "Who feels like doing this?" Answer: not too many. To repeat a main theme of this book, you don't have to feel like doing something to do it. A few questions, even if tentative, can send the message "OK, I'm suspending my verbal offensive—or defensive—and trying to understand you."

If you are honestly asking someone to clarify, he may settle his tone. He will be less prone to continue a barrage. Put another way, it's harder to build a case when one keeps getting guided back to why he is building his case.

Resistance Rationale #1: "I don't know what to ask."

Welcome to my world. I ask questions for a living, and sometimes I don't know what to ask or when or how. Using questions skillfully is a process, for the professional and the beginner. Some people start out instinctively good at it and get better. Others stumble forward through trial and error. Either way, improvement comes with the asking.

The fundamental question to ask is *why?* "Why do you think that?" "Why are you upset?" "Why do you think I do this?" Nothing fancy, just a basic request for elaboration.

A few more standards are:

> What do I do that makes you say (think, feel) that?
> In what ways do I give you that impression?
> Where and when do I do that most?
> When do I come across that way?
> How often do you think this?

You may or may not garner a thoughtful answer, and we'll get to that shortly. Still, your questions in and of themselves make a statement: "I want to know what's in your head."

As I told my son Jon, the asking part is fairly easy. Almost any personal revelation can prompt questions from every direction. If, however, one assumes battle posture at the first sound of negativity from his spouse, the inclination to dispute overrides the desire to understand. If I think that what you think stinks, I'm not disposed to ask much about it.

Fortunately, "I don't know what to ask" is readily overcome. Humans are naturally curious creatures. They want answers. The instinct will return if allowed.

Resistance Rationale #2: "He doesn't know the answer."

Every parent knows acutely the futility of probing a child's head to fathom why he did what he did. What could possibly have possessed Blade to carve his initials into the neighbor's vinyl siding? And the agitation only mounts after receiving the ever-ready explanation, "I don't know," or the ever more communicative blank stare, as if to say, "What's vinyl siding? Whose initials? We have neighbors?"

The story goes that a young boy approaches his father. "Dad, why is the sky so blue?"

"That's a good question, Son. I really don't know."

"Well, what makes clouds have different shapes?"

"I've wondered about that myself."

"Do you think the sun will ever burn out?"

"I suppose it could."

"Dad?"

"Huh?"

"Do you mind my asking you all these questions?"

"Of course not, Son. How else will you ever learn anything?"

Just because a question is well put and well timed does not mean it will be rewarded with a well-thought-out answer. Just because something is good to do doesn't mean it always works.

Early personality theories stressed gaining insight or an awareness of one's own underlying motives and struggles. Freud asserted that without insight, cure was, if not impossible, highly unlikely. Reality offers added insights to Freud:

- One, you can be acutely aware of the why of your conduct and still not change that conduct.
- Two, insight is not always desired, particularly if you're human. Have you ever in exasperation said, "Can't he see what he's like?" "Isn't she the least bit aware of how she comes across?" "How can he observe that fault so clearly in everybody else and be blind to it in himself?" What is obvious to you about another may not be so obvious to him. And being asked about it takes him onto alien psychological turf. He simply hasn't spent much time living there or wanting to live there.

The author C.S. Lewis said that an idea seldom seemed so unclear to him as after he had just defended it. Your spouse may not be much inclined to self-scrutiny in marital matters. He may need a little time to trust that you're not trying to trick or trap him and that you truly want to know. But unless he's emotionally stuck at three years old , he does have the innate capacity to show flashes of insight.

So don't be discouraged if upon your first question you get little enlightening feedback. If I were to be deterred by silence or confusion in response to my best counselor-type queries, some of my sessions would end ten minutes after starting.

Resistance Rationale #3: "I'm afraid of the answers."
Some spouses won't provide any sort of answer to a question you've posed twenty-two times. Others will repeat themselves twenty-two times when you didn't even ask to hear it once. I'm not sure which style is more unsettling.

Small step #3, "Listen a Minute," carries the resistance that self-imposed silence will only open oneself to more criticism.

If you don't promptly defend yourself, who knows what more you'll be charged with? While silence is a passive response, tacitly allowing the speaker to head where his thoughts and words take him, questioning is an active response. It purposely elicits further explanation for whatever negatives are coming out. In a sense that makes questioning more risky than listening. Whereas one says, "Go on. I'm listening," the other says, "Tell me more specifically why you think badly of me or our situation."

Likely you know, at least in part, why your spouse thinks badly. How much of what you hear is brand new? How much of it is old stuff that you don't want to hear again? In other words, you may not like her answers, but some of them you could put into words yourself, perhaps in more detail.

Then again, suppose what pours forth is new and disturbing. That you're just now hearing it in no way means it hasn't been brewing for some time. Commonly people resist visiting a doctor when something seems wrong because they don't want to know exactly what it could be. As long as the ailment remains indefinite, it can be pushed out of mind (until too bad to ignore).

Your questions will help to clarify the problem. What you're asking to hear may be hard to hear. Having it revealed some other way, perhaps through harsh words, passive resistance, or manipulation, will be harder. Asking at your time and pace gives you some control over when it does reveal itself. Every physician will tell you, the earlier the diagnosis is made, the better.

Resistance Rationale #4: "I already know what I'm going to hear."

If you're a parent, no doubt you've reiterated the same themes of character and moral instruction in similar words, hundreds and perhaps thousands of times. And your child isn't yet in first grade.

In family therapy I will ask a youngster to please explain why Mom or Dad disciplines for a particular offense. At which he will launch into an adultlike account of his parents' motives and rationale. After the parents recover from their stunned "How did he know that?" look, I observe that little Sherlock has likely heard them tell him "that" dozens of times per month of age. It sunk in, intellectually at least.

As an aside, the accuracy of a child's insight is not necessarily related to his age. Some of the younger ones out-explain the teens. That could be because the teens aren't about to reveal anything they know that we think they don't.

With what accuracy do you know what you're going to hear? My experience—both in counseling and my marriage—is that just when I think my understanding is complete, I discover more I didn't know. Repeatedly I see that my knowledge about another and her ways is not as informed as I thought. More can be learned.

Should you already know in full what you're going to hear, shift your motive for asking. Seek less to understand and more to avoid conflict. A question or two, like an "I'm sorry" and a one-minute listen, can delay, even short-circuit, the "Oh, yeah, what about you?" template of many arguments.

Seldom have I heard any spouse repel a sincere question with, "Why are you asking me that? You've heard me before. I'm not about to tell you again." When someone is voicing a grievance, she's not about to stop voicing it just because she's being asked to elaborate. She may think by now that, if you've been attending at all, you should know. But like any typical parent, if she has to repeat herself, she will.

Resistance Rationale #5: "I'd get accused of interrogating."

Recall the parenting program that warned, "Don't ask questions. That is a form of interrogation"? Apparently some expert types would agree with this resistance rationale.

This begs the question, "Is any questioning at all an interrogation?" The answer, it seems, would hinge on the tone and phrasing of the question. "So you think you're the only one in this house whose feelings get hurt?" carries a far more accusatory punch than "How did I hurt you by saying that? What do you think I meant?"

Emphasis and demeanor are so powerful that they can give identical wording an opposite impact. "Do you *really* believe I think that?" imparts something quite different from "Do you really believe I think *that*?" The former conveys challenging disbelief; the latter asks for more clarification.

Within a disagreement, questions can be used to dispute: "How in heaven's name did you come to that conclusion?" "What possesses you to act so surly in front of my relatives?" "Do you realize how you came across last night?" These are provocations—not questions but assertions. There is little intent to get more information. Calling such an interrogation would be the nicest way to characterize it.

Couldn't an interrogation snowball from the sheer number of queries? One, maybe several, wouldn't be excessive, but couldn't a rapid-fire string of why, what, when, and where irritate another or grow tiresome? It depends. (Can shrinks ever give a definitive answer? How'd you like to be married to one of us?)

Some pages back I presented the illustration of a person who, upon first impression, appealed to you as immediately likeable. She kept the conversation directed at you, mostly by asking all about you. Her interest was obvious and sincere. Did you have to stifle an urge to counter with, "Why are you asking so many questions? What is this, some kind of third degree?" I suspect not. You were flattered. The "relentless" questions added to a total effect: I really want to know about you.

One question posed with disdain is far more threatening than twenty posed with genuine concern. The numbers do not define an interrogation; the style does.

Resistance Rationale #6: "I don't believe the explanation."

Of all the resistance rationales, this one is the most resistant. It has the potential to abruptly disrupt any exchange, however amicably begun, and propel it directly into verbal combat. It declares, "No matter what your answer, I am not moved nor even interested." Or worse, "You lie."

Challenging this rationale is so critical to improving a marriage that it will receive its own chapter next.

Question Scenario

Wife: I think we need to talk.

Husband: What about this time?

Therapist: That's a question but not a good one. It's sarcastic, and it attempts to put Wife on the defensive. Its message is "Here we go again." Try a different question.

Husband: Why do you think so?

Therapist: Why? is a natural opener, much more effective with a good tone.

Wife: Well, first of all, last night is the last night I will ever ask you to help me in front of your buddies.

Husband: What did I do?

Wife: What did you do!? Do you even have to ask that?

Therapist: Hubby may only be seeking more details in order to find out how best to defend himself. Even if not, sometimes the most agreeable requests get rebuffed with an implicit, "What are you, some kind of idiot?"

Husband: No, I really want to know. What exactly did I do to make you feel bad?

Wife: You did what you always do. You're willing to help when it's just the two of us. But as soon as your friends are around, you have to be Mr. Bossman of the house. No woman is going to order you around.

Therapist: Here is the most likely place for the conversation to go sour, as the personal attacks are mounting. Nonetheless, Husband still has time to assuage.

Husband: I'm sorry. I don't really mean to come across like that. It's a bad habit.

Therapist: Mixing and matching the various small steps has a synergistic effect. Each makes the others more settling.

Wife: You're d*** right, it's a bad habit. And you don't seem to even care how bad it makes me look.

Therapist: When a spouse is feeling neglected or mistreated, contrition or an honest question won't always soothe. Sometimes it takes a few more.

Husband: What can I do next time so you aren't put in that spot again?

Therapist: A great question. It asks, "How in your eyes can I do better?" It can alter the course of the whole interchange.

Wife: Maybe you could just not have your buddies over anymore while I'm home.

Therapist: Not all ends well every time. This time around there was no meeting of the minds or hearts.

Two positives did happen though. One, the argument didn't turn as nasty as it might have. Two, Husband planted a few seeds for next time. His different style will sound a little less different.

One final question, from Wife.

Wife: What have you been reading? *Marriage for Dummies?*

The Last Word

There is no shortage of how-to communication manuals out there. Some reiterate common sense. Others stretch far for new and enlightened modes of "interface." All can run the risk of sounding artificial, evoking the question, "Who actually talks like that?"

Asking honest questions of another is the standard stuff of communication. It always has been. It takes little special training or savvy. Even if the first few faltering questions don't initially evoke good answers, they are still good in themselves. It's hard to feel and fuel upset with someone who's temporarily ceased pushing his point and is trying to receive yours.

The irony is, if you want to get another to accept your side, argue less and ask more.

| *Accept It* |

Accept what? Life as it is? Marriage as it's been? Verbal put-downs? An excuse? A lie? Just what does "Accept It" mean?

In its broad sense, "Accept It" is a wise philosophy for living. Much of life—the past, other people, adverse circumstances—can't be altered, not directly anyway. Thus, like it or not, for our own psychological well-being, we must accept it.

Most of us know this. It's advice we first heard as preschoolers. Transferring it to our hearts and emotions, however, is the schooling of a lifetime.

A good definition of frustration: the difference between the way we'd like things or people to be and the way they are. The greater the gap between our desires and reality, the greater the frustration. To reduce frustration, therefore, adjusting our attitude is a good course, generally easier than adjusting life itself.

Within a marriage two people meshing distinct histories, personalities, and perceptions must develop a healthy amount of acceptance—sometimes tolerance—for each other. It's absolutely key to getting along well. To deny acceptance is to accept frustration. Discerning what to accept, when, and for how long, though, is the crux of the matter.

To clarify what "Accept It" is, let's first clarify what it is not. It is not permitting abuse. It is not overlooking wrong. It is not believing a lie. It is not agreeing to an obvious contradiction. It is not making oneself vulnerable to manipulation.

What then does "Accept It" mean? It means that during a conversation or argument (the when), you will not immediately (the how long) dispute your spouse's thinking or motive (the what). Perhaps you're objecting that this step is neither small nor easy (and I'll accept that). It strikes straight at the heart of your disagreements. You don't always believe or trust what the other is saying. How do you get past your own suspicions?

An illustration: Your spouse has just surprised you with her decision not to attend an upcoming family get-together. Your opinionated sister will be there, and your wife says she's about had her fill of the snide side comments about her motherhood. Your first urge might be to counter with something like, "I've never heard her say that much. Besides, you know my sister. She talks too much. You can't take her personally." In so many words, "I don't accept what you're saying." The base for an argument is now laid.

You may not agree with your wife's decision. You may believe it's a flimsy justification for spending less time with your family. You may suspect her insecurity is talking. Nonetheless, at this early juncture restrain your comebacks. Don't contest her reasoning. Let her make her case, and then consider her case.

"Why do you think my sister does that?" Or, "Did she say anything the last time we were together?" Implicitly you've accepted her motive, however wrongheaded you think it is, leaving you better positioned to resolve the impasse. "What if I stay close to you during dinner? Is that when she says things?" Or, "If I hear one rude comment, we'll both move to another room."

To sidestep brewing trouble, sometimes you have to flow with the other person's thinking. If you immediately challenge it, you could meet with defensiveness, silence, or volume.

Throughout therapy I must be prepared to accept what I'm being told. For example, a husband claims his wife is hard to please, constantly trying to control his every move. I, on the other hand, have formed a different impression. I see him as having minimal tolerance for anyone, especially a wife, reminding him of his husbandly and fatherly responsibilities. Her "controlling" is more his reaction to being asked to do anything he disagrees with.

Suppose I aim to summarily straighten him out with the likes of "Is your wife too controlling, or do you want to answer to no one?" As therapeutically on target as that might be, what is the likelihood I'll be rewarded with "Golly, Dr. Ray, what an insightful response to my own self-serving rationale. I can tell you have a PH.D.!"?

For the sake of progress, I'll do better not to debate his thinking just yet. After spending more time exploring it, I'll be more credible when I do challenge it, perhaps from a different angle.

Many marital clashes fit a similar template: Wife offers an observation or opinion. Husband doesn't agree. Wife restates her position. Husband argues why it's even more wrong. Wife offers additional reasons. Husband considers those reasons illegitimate or foolish. Wife feels compelled to defend her personhood. The initial issue is now buried, covered by a mutual mistrust of meaning and motives.

"Accept it" redirects an interchange getting thus bogged down. It only takes one person to acknowledge, if not in mind then in words, the other's perspective. The course of the argument then shifts from that of "I think…," "No, you don't" to "OK, what makes you think that?"

Notice that a little acceptance is tied to small step #4, "Ask a Few Questions." Most of us aren't inclined to ask anything further about something we believe is outright untrustworthy. If we reject its legitimacy, why seek to understand it? The matter, in our minds, deserves neither acceptance nor clarification.

Resistance Rationale #1: "I can't accept something that is obviously wrong."

You don't have to accept that two plus two equals five. Nor that the earth is flat. Accepting something someone says does not require unquestioningly abiding mangled facts or a clear warping of the truth. To paraphrase a social philosopher, everyone is entitled to his own opinion; he is not entitled to his own facts.

Scenario: Your husband claims he did take the trash to the curb, as you asked two days ago. One brief glance (and whiff) into the garage reveals four overflowing trash bags spewing bacterial biomass. Maybe what he meant was that he did haul out two of the six bags. And maybe you're unwilling to start a fracas over the exact number of bags that constitutes "the trash." That doesn't mean you must deny your senses. Nor offer an "Oops, my mistake, Dear. I see you did indeed take care of the garbage as you define it," all the while wobbling down the driveway with two bags under each arm. Silence may be the better option, but it doesn't imply agreement.

Sometimes letting pass minor misstatements of fact is smart. Otherwise you could become embroiled in a habitual and agitating type of spousal interaction: bickering.

Husband: I can't believe I got the lawn mowed before dark.

Wife: It's been dark for twenty minutes, and you just walked in here.

Husband: It wasn't totally dark. I could still see where I was going.

Wife: How? You would have been done an hour ago if you'd have started at 3:00, like you said you were going to.

Husband: I did. I walked into the garage a few minutes after 3:00.

Wife: A few minutes after 3:00? I don't know how you tell time, but the kitchen clock said 3:43 when that mower started up.

Husband: That's because the mower didn't start up right away, and I had to put gas in it.

Wife: It always starts up the first time. You said that's why you like it. Besides, I looked right at the clock when the mower started, and it was no more than three minutes after you walked outside.

Husband: It couldn't have been only three minutes. It takes longer than that to get the mower out of the garage.

Wife: Well, maybe it wouldn't take so long if you kept the garage cleaned up.

The only thing more irritating than reading this sort of verbal grappling is participating in it. Or listening to it, as the two pugilists spar over daylight, clocks, and mowers. Chronic bickerers can become so domesticated in their style that they are only slightly, if at all, aware of how uncomfortable it makes anyone within earshot.

What drives bickering? The need to correct. It is the unwillingness to accept another's facts. How crucial is it to pinpoint the exact time someone walked out the door and started the mower? Why the desire to prove each detail? Especially given that 82.64

percent of the time—my informal assessment—neither person budges from his or her view of the world. With little resolved, the argument either winds down from fatigue or flares into more sensitive matters than a lawn.

Disputed minutiae provide the grist for the verbal grinding. Don't argue each and every point of fact, and you dramatically erode the base for bickering. Can you accept this?

In life, as in bickering, so often perception is reality. A wife will seek therapy with me because of depression. Several sessions make it apparent that at the heart of her depression is marital discord. At my request her husband begins to attend couples counseling. Having already heard her describe the marriage, I subsequently listen to her husband.

The pictures presented come not from two people living in the same household or even in the same state. The two people would appear to reside on different planets. Their views of the relationship are so disparate as to make uncovering the "real marriage" quite a winding journey. Usually neither is deliberately offering a false view of the other—in other words, a lie. They are manifesting a profoundly human trait: seeing life and others through a highly personal lens. In itself that isn't bad, so long as one recognizes that the lens can sometimes be clouded or distorted.

Once more, accept some minor "wrong" facts. You'll keep trivial exchanges from flaring into full-blown conflicts. Also, as we shall next see in more detail, what sounds clearly incorrect may mainly be an outlook different from yours.

Resistance Rationale #2: "I don't believe what I'm hearing."

This rationale sounds similar to the one previous. Closer scrutiny reveals a key difference. Resistance Rationale #1 is the unwillingness to accept a statement that is contradicted by the facts. Resistance Rationale #2 is the reluctance to accept a statement that, while hard to believe, may in fact be true.

Often I'm asked, "How can you tell if someone in counseling is lying to you?" My answer: I can't—not always or easily anyway. Detecting contradictions or inconsistencies, particularly subtle ones, can take time. Even when initially skeptical, I have to reserve judgment. Sometimes my early doubts are confirmed; other times what I was slow to accept shows itself to be authentic.

A fascinating study analyzed how and when clinicians determined a diagnosis. It uncovered the tendency to diagnose early, often during the first visit. Once formed, the diagnosis stayed formed, modifying ever so slowly, if at all, to fit with any new, contradictory information.

A similar phenomenon occurs in marriage. If one partner concludes that the other is not being totally honest in some matter, that attitude solidifies quickly. With each related disagreement it grows stronger. "I didn't buy it the first time I heard it, and I don't buy it now." Early judgments resist alteration, seriously hampering a resolution.

Let's say that the children's bedtime has been a sore spot between you and your husband. Before leaving for the evening to run errands, therefore, you make sure he looks you straight in the face and recites the mutually established bedtime, and to seal the deal, you add a kiss. Confident that this time he'll follow through, you stay out an extra hour, planning on returning to some couple quiet time.

You return home to find all three children (two kids and one husband) eating popcorn and watching TV an hour and a half past bedtime. You could have overlooked a half hour, maybe forty-five minutes, but an hour and a half, on a school night, for a first grader with a cold? Confronting your husband calmly, so as not to disturb the children's snacking, you receive "Oh, wow. I never realized it was this late. I totally forgot about their bedtime."

You have two options, (three, if you count firing a warning shot with a bazooka two feet over your husband's head). One, instantly dismantle his excuse. "Oh, yes. I'm sure you totally forgot. For nearly two hours it just kept slipping your mind." At which point you could hear, "It did slip my mind. The kids and I were enjoying the movie. They'll be fine tomorrow." Keep pushing for an admission, and you'll hear more variants of the same defense.

As unnatural as it might feel, consider option two. Accept the fact that, even though you're little persuaded, you can't know for certain if his explanation is legitimate. Granted, it smells fishy, and indeed, you've heard similar fish stories before, but what will you hear if you keep pursuing the matter? "Gee, Sweetheart, you're absolutely right, as usual. I didn't forget. I just needed to concoct some flimsy excuse to keep a fight from brewing at this late hour. It would keep the children awake, you know."

You needn't believe your spouse's rationale 100 percent in order to sidestep a clash. How about 50 percent? 25 percent? OK, how about 10 percent? Could it be a little trustworthy? How do you prove it's not? Just as you realize you can't, so too does he. Another's internal state, emotional or cognitive, is exceptionally difficult to challenge, particularly if he doesn't want it challenged. In so many words, you're giving the benefit of the doubt.

Have you ever confessed to another, "I'm sorry," and received some version of "No, you're not"? Trying to convince, "Yes, I truly am," you meet more skepticism. Your gesture is genuine, but you meet, in effect, "That's baloney," or "Yeah, right." Checkmate.

Rejecting another person's reasons or motives doesn't always convey, "I don't believe you." It sometimes implies, "You're a liar." Not too many accusations arouse ire more quickly than being called, however phrased, a liar. And whether or not one actually is lying, the charge ignites hot words. Often it's better to accept something that, at best, sounds minimally legitimate and to angle it toward a solution.

So how do you solve the bedtime bad time? This evening you can't. Your focus is on the future. Accepting the "I forgot" this time means better preparation next time Mr. Responsible is asked to do something as complex as checking a clock. Perhaps you could call home at bedtime to "remind him" or come back a little earlier if convenient. Before leaving, in addition to making him repeat the bedtime out loud, you could write it on his forehead, in indelible ink, placing a notarized copy in your attorney's office. Or you could do what my wife has done: pay the oldest child ten dollars to babysit Dad for the evening.

You don't need to believe a statement fully to accept it. What percentage of personal doubt you endure before you question is, of course, your decision. Keep in mind though that even the most experienced therapists find that determining someone's internal state is tricky at best and at worst can badly mislead.

Resistance Rationale #3: "I refuse to look foolish."

Every small step in this book so far has encountered a resistance rationale that asserts, in effect, "I won't be played for a dummy." Deep within most of us, something strongly opposes looking naïve, gullible, or stupid. Some experts would label this an "ego defense mechanism." Indeed, it does have psychological value. It's not healthy to allow oneself to be victimized.

The downside to this mindset is that we can slip into a self-protective hypervigilance. That is, "No one had better try to outwit me; I'm ready for any kind of verbal trickery." Unfortunately, such wariness can ensnare us in a relational style that's overfocused on self-defense and not focused enough on seeking accord.

Suppose your spouse claims his sole reason for wanting to get together with four single friends every other Friday night at Cruiser's Sports Bar is their great lattes. Most likely you wouldn't deny your own instincts and credulously swallow his explanation. When facing obvious manipulation—though the meanings of *obvious* and *manipulation* vary widely from spouse to spouse—you needn't worry about looking the fool because you're not about to be the fool.

Many if not most marriage trouble spots are not so clear-cut. They are wrapped in shades of gray. Determining whether or not you are being buffaloed isn't all that easy. You may suspect so, but you can't be sure. You must make a judgment. Would it be better to keep intact your self-image as a savvy reader of psyches, or would it be better to risk looking gullible for the sake of peace or some resolution?

Scenario: For the third night in a row, after coming home from work, you've prepared supper for the family. Your wife claims she has simply been too busy with computer projects to get to it. As a stay-at-home mom, she constructs her daily schedule, and you are well aware that whatever computer demands press upon her, they are minimal compared to her time spent e-mailing, social networking, and web browsing.

You could declare, "Of course. I'm shocked that in only five hours on the computer, you managed to catch up on your e-mails *and* update your *My Face* site. What was I thinking?"

Your sarcasm makes it plain that you are not buying her argument. It also makes plain your argument. "Who do you think you're talking to? One of the kids?"

At one level you've protected yourself. On another you've undercut yourself, turning from your goal: getting supper on the table despite the computer's siren call.

What are your options? Will your wife agree to prepare supper an hour later? Can you bring supper home two nights a week? Can you ask your wife, "Can you get your computer work done tonight so we can have a family supper tomorrow night?" When calmer can you both revisit the issue?

Granted, the options may sound naïve, implying, "OK, I'll let you feed me this computer baloney for now." But they also plot a course: "Where do we go from here?"

What if, in fact, your spouse rests assured that she did fool you and that doing so was childishly easy? Her self-assurance is false. You weren't fooled. You made a strategic and adult calculation. Despite looking temporarily outmaneuvered, you aimed to break the dead-end pattern of, "Let me see if you'll believe this," countered by, "Don't feed me that line. I'm on to you."

One more complication of Resistance Rationale #3: It may move your spouse to cling more tenaciously to her answers, as she is not about to look the fool either. If she accepts your accusations, she allows you to corner her. She looks insincere, and nobody likes being so viewed. The communication is at loggerheads.

But if she thinks you can be fooled once, why wouldn't she try to fool you twice, or twenty times? Let's consider that.

Resistance Rationale #4: "If my spouse can fool me one time, why wouldn't he try again?"

A little folk ditty says, "Fool me once, shame on you. Fool me twice, shame on me." Said another way, it's bad enough to be a one-time victim; it's much worse to assume the role.

This worry can be eased several ways.

- First, to reserve judgment does not mean to suspend judgment. Eventually the need to dispute your spouse's thinking may assert itself. The plan is to delay that urge beyond first suspicions. The stronger relationships do.

  For example, you doubt that your spouse is "too tired" to tackle a dripping faucet. Despite making the claim three times in the past two days, within an hour he was pursuing some activity. Twice it was golf. His dodges aside, you've learned that the project eventually will get addressed, so for now you decide not to plumb this problem, though hearing "I'm tired" is getting tiresome, and you may confront it after his next golf outing.

- Second, what you think is false may actually be true, if only a little. While your husband denies feeling "mean" when he disciplines the children, to you he clearly sounds upset. Despite his decibel level, is it possible he is not feeling so angry as you think? His repeated denials may not be attempts to trick your ears. They may be his way of reinforcing, "I honestly don't feel that mean." Repetition may or may not indicate serial deception.

  Third, when trusting someone with little or no emotional tie to you, a degree of caution may be warranted. On the other hand, a marriage is composed of two people in a relationship (or a residual history of one). Therefore, if one hopes to better that relationship, she does well to keep in check an attitude of "I'll give you one chance to be straight with me. Then you're done." Closer relationships deserve more chances.

Finally, even in better marriages, the benefit of the doubt can be exhausted. A spouse who incessantly offers the same explanation, against accumulating evidence to the contrary, will lose credibility. His once accommodating partner will no longer be manipulated. Said simply, most people can only be fooled for so long.

Whether you're being fooled once or more, you'll eventually know it. In the meantime, discerning for certain could be tough. To get to the truth underlying a trouble spot, it might be smart to play dumb for a little while.

Accept It Scenario

Wife: Why is it that you wait to discipline the kids until you get mad? You get fed up and then you blow.

Husband: I don't wait until I'm fed up. I discipline when they actually do something wrong.

Therapist: Dad could have immediately short-circuited this exchange by acknowledging, not necessarily agreeing with, his wife's observation. Instead, within two sentences, things are moving toward "No, I don't," "Yes, you do."

Wife: You may discipline them when they do something wrong, but you tolerate about ten misbehaviors before you do anything. So they get away with a lot while you're getting to your boiling point.

Husband: I overlook a lot because you overlook little. Somebody has to let them be kids.

Therapist: Neither is considering the other's viewpoint, so what began as a disagreement over "facts" is getting personal. Hubby took the focus of the fracas off himself and aimed it directly back at his wife—at her motherhood, no less. She's not about to permit that.

Wife: Oh, so now I'm the reason for your poor discipline. It isn't your laziness; it's my witchiness.

Husband: I didn't say you were a witch. I said you get on them a lot. Sometimes you just have to let things go. I do because I don't want to be on them constantly.

Therapist: Husband did make a backhanded attempt at an apology, trying to correct his wife's misconstruing of his words. Nevertheless, he still excuses himself by claiming he doesn't want to be like his wife, who in his eyes, and by implication the kids', is the truly intolerant one.

Wife: You do this all the time. Somehow everything gets turned back on me. I'm the meanie, while good-time Disney Dad has to protect the kids from me. I don't buy that garbage for a minute. You don't discipline because you're oblivious half the time to what they're doing.

Husband: I notice more than you think. Just because I don't always do something doesn't mean I don't see it. I just think it's better to let some stuff pass.

Therapist: Dad has reiterated his reasoning three times: "I don't act because I think you act too much." Mom disputes it each time she hears it. Also, she probably fears that if she accepts any part of it as legitimate, her self-image as a mother will be threatened. So she resists.

Wife: Don't give me that. If you think it's better to let some misbehavior go, why are you so mad when you finally do act like a father?

Therapist: Ouch. If he's going to impugn her motherhood, she'll impugn his fatherhood. The fighting can get dirty when neither person is willing to acknowledge what the other thinks. Mom can better get to the root of Dad's sloppy discipline by curtailing her insistence that he's foisting a bogus explanation on her. Let me put the words in her mouth.

Wife: What do you think I do that is so hard on the kids?

Husband: You're on them all the time—nagging, reminding, arguing. I don't argue. I say it once, and then I act.

Therapist: Mom is thinking, "What planet are you raising the kids on? You're delusional." But if she voices this, the argument again regresses. Allow me to write her script. That's easy for me; I'm not emotionally involved here.

Wife: Do you think I don't discipline at all or that I talk too much?

Husband: No, you do discipline, but you overtalk, too. That's why I ignore some things. I don't want to add to all the words.

Therapist: The inflaming revelation is that Dad rationalizes his discipline style as a compensation for Mom's. Not concurring one bit, Mom is ready to go on the offense to defend herself. When feeling personally attacked, it's hard to find any validity in another's arguments.

One course correction would be for Dad to yield some ground. But because he didn't like Mom's initial tone, he too immediately went into self-protective mode. So what's the resolution?

Wife: I'm sorry. I realize from what you're saying that I could do a far better job of disciplining consistently. Sometimes deep down I do admire your way of parenting, and I feel inferior.

Husband: That's all right, Sweetheart. No apology needed. You've helped me recognize that, in my own way, I'm just as inconsistent, if not more so than I accuse you of being. In the future let's agree to help each other past our own weaknesses, for our sakes and the kids'.

Therapist: OK, what planet do I live on? I just couldn't resist scripting this like some pop-psychology article, implying that if only spouses would communicate in the maritally correct manner, the sky would clear, the birds would sing, and the "Hallelujah Chorus" would burst forth.

Returning to reality, whatever the chances for some meeting of the minds, both spouses would benefit from trying to hear what the other is saying. Pardon the slip into psychobabble; I, too, read magazines. Temporarily setting aside the defense of the self for the sake of peace or resolution is no doubt a big challenge. But the reward is bigger: a more respectful marriage and a more respected self.

The Last Word

One reality governs most disagreements: If even one contestant replaces arguing with the unspoken, "I'll acknowledge your side, and though I think it's pretty weak, I'll try to understand it," the contest loses momentum.

Temporarily accepting another's viewpoint might mean accepting a little more personal blame than you'd like. But there is a payoff. Believe it or not, he may relent and accept a little blame too. Put the mirror on yourself, and your spouse may see his own reflection more clearly.

| *Dump the* D *Word* |

All parents, except those with no children, say things they shouldn't. Ugly words piggyback on heated emotions, even if regretted at the very moment they're making themselves heard. Like a slow motion scene from an old movie, the lines tumble out in what appears to be an unstoppable stream resisting our flailing efforts to pull them back.

Who of us hasn't fired off sentiments at our kids that we'd never to anyone else, save perhaps our spouse? If we did spout off to other family members and friends, we might soon find only our kids and spouse left to talk to. Anyone else would make distance between us and our mouth.

In defense of moms and dads everywhere, the kids do play a major role in our overuse of words and misuse of emotions. Commonly they don't react until we overreact. "Go ahead, Taylor, leave your dress bunched up under your bed again, and you won't get another one until your wedding day, and I won't pay for it!" "How do I know you're not telling me the truth, Linus? Your lips are moving." "Hazel, you have two hours to clean and fumigate this room, or your new residence is the shed, and not our shed either."

A hallmark of addiction is tolerance. More of the same stuff is needed to get the same effect. Over time the effect decreases.

A parallel can be drawn to social interactions. Anger and threats can rattle another into submission or good behavior. With repetition though, they lose impact or, worse, breed resistance and hostility.

Distressed couples come to my office seeking to heal their married life, but should that prove too hard, always lurking in the distance is the divorce door. It's been cracked open, periodically or routinely in the past, when marital dissatisfaction has reached a certain pitch. If the discontent ebbs and flows, the attraction toward leaving ebbs and flows. All too often though, even in the better times, it lingers, as one or both spouses anticipates the return of worse times.

As disharmony persists, the temptation to fantasize about escape persists. What would life be like free of the frustration, the sadness, the sense of neglect? To not have to work so hard just to get along passably? Just as little people shoot off, "I'm running away," when facing unwanted limits or expectations, bigger people, while not always voicing the desire, may think, *Run.*

Saying the *D* word aloud the first time is, fortunately, hard for most spouses. It is a verbal threshold over which they're reluctant to talk or walk. It has a harshness, a scary, life-changing sound. As a result many remain uneasy with the unadulterated term. Instead they hint at it through euphemism. "Maybe we should think about our future together." "It is just getting too hard to work at this every day." "Do you want to live like this until we're seventy-five?"

Call it the *D* thought. While not as emotionally slamming as the word itself, it does dance around the idea. It brings to mind separation as a possibility, one that can increase as it's pondered. Once the thought is conceived, the word, indeed the deed, has grounds to root. Divorce has entered the realm of real.

Parents ask me, "What if I've finally realized how poor my discipline has been for years? Is it too late to change?" Often the question comes from parents who have long been lax, permissive, or erratic. I answer, "Whether in fact it turns out to be too late or not, you must act as though it's not. You must begin to reverse what's been happening up until now. You must stop the downward trend."

So it is with the *D* word. If it or some synonym has wormed its way into your marriage and is eating away at your commitment, it's never too late to crush it. No matter its damage so far, you can still act to halt any further ill effects. Before healing begins, the virus has to be destroyed.

If your physician advised you to stop eating anything containing wheat, as it is slowly destroying your small intestine, would you reply, "How about if I just gradually cut back over the next year or two? Do I have to quit all at once?" He'd likely retort, "If you want to immediately halt the damage, reverse it, and give yourself time to heal, you have no choice. But if you're not all that worried about illness and possible death, eat what you want."

A qualification: As observed in my earliest pages, some marriages are seriously disturbed. They are dangerous to the safety or well-being of a spouse or children. Or for any number of personal justifications, one spouse is absolutely determined to abandon the marriage. Here, tragically so, divorce may be an intruder who can't be subdued.

In the majority of divorce-threatened marriages, however, the core dynamic is two people progressively drifting apart, or getting along poorly, or flat out disliking each other. The relationship still has strengths upon which to build. It is not irretrievably or irreparably damaged, though it might seem so. These are the marriages that I'm referring to as I propose small step #6, "Dump the *D* Word."

Resistance Rationale #1: "I just don't see anything getting better."

Far more people think about suicide than actually follow through. Studies consistently reveal one mind-set behind the act: hopelessness. It's not that the person wants to die; he just doesn't want to live. The immediate therapeutic focus with someone contemplating suicide is to give him hope or the sense that, as long as he is alive, change is possible; what's more, it's likely.

Suicide has been called a permanent solution to a temporary problem. Meaning, the act is the ultimate in finality, pursued because one is convinced the pain is permanent. There will be no let-up. The only way to lessen it is to leave it.

This is the sense of many in depressing marriages. How long will this go on? How long can I endure it? Once again, the solution, divorce, is more or less permanent to the problem of pain, which may or may not be permanent.

Practicing psychology has revealed to me certain "megathemes" of life. A foremost is that change is certain. Even if one does little or nothing to alter a bad situation, things will change, somehow, some way, in time. Nothing involving human beings is static. We and our problems are ever in flux.

The spouse who thinks, "I don't want a divorce, but I see no other end to all this," has effectively concluded no change at all will ever happen. The only course will be downward. This is not the inevitable reality. It may feel like the reality. It may be the reality one has faced for years. But to accept it means to give up on all possibilities other than the one that asserts, "My spouse will never be any different or treat me any better."

Such a surrender must be challenged. If one is glancing toward divorce with all its added complications and wholesale life alterations, she needs to be as sure as can be that it is the preferred option and that, in fact, no others exist. That is an extremely shaky conclusion, given the unknowns that define much of the future.

Even if you do nothing other than you always have, life will alter its direction. Should you determine to act differently, you dramatically raise the prospect that the future will be unlike the past. In essence, that's the message of this whole book: The most minor of personal improvements can reap major rewards.

The joke goes that an elderly farmer and his wife were sitting in a church service when suddenly a vile, sulfur-smelling creature exploded onto the scene. People screamed in panic and ran toward the doors—all except the farmer, who sat unperturbed.

The creature did his best, and without success, to terrorize this last congregant, hissing, "Do you know who I am?"

"Yep."

"Aren't you scared?"

"Nope."

"Why not?"

"Been living with your sister for forty years."

Unless you've been living with Satan or his sister, which I highly doubt, change yourself for the better, and your spouse will become better to live with, even if inch by erratic inch. Previously we emphasized that if you want compliments, give them. The marital parallel is, if you want a spouse to change, change yourself.

"But I have changed, and still it makes no difference." I don't always know how completely accurate that assertion is when I hear it. I do know this: We typically see ourselves as less in need of fixing than others. For most of us there is room for work, and whatever little we do could have a noticeable effect on those around us.

Those who believe that little or nothing will improve their domestic lot have given up on the future helping them or on themselves helping the future. They've come to believe divorce is the answer to an unsolvable question. Indeed, it is an answer, but it may be one built upon a false conclusion about life and people.

Resistance Rationale #2: "I wasn't first to use the D word."

During the Cold War both the United States and the Soviet Union adhered to a concept called "mutually assured destruction" or MAD. If either country were to initiate a nuclear attack, the other would retaliate with like nuclear force, thus guaranteeing massive destruction for both countries. This prospect, it was said, in large part kept all from launching a first strike.

Divorce is the nuclear option in a warring marriage. Typically both partners don't threaten such high-level action concurrently. Most of the time one person launches the first salvo, rocking the other hard emotionally. The other then responds in kind, or as it were, in unkind, thus ultimately risking a form of MAD, *maritally* assured destruction.

The temptation to fight fire with fire can be overwhelming. Such is how most conflicts escalate into conflagrations. If one side would restrain the impulse to return hurt for hurt and threat for threat, the odds of heavy destruction for both sides would dramatically lessen.

There are multiple reasons not to meet D word with D word. First, someone acting badly toward us offers no justification to do likewise. We may believe so, but if something is wrong, it is no less wrong for us to do because we didn't do it first. One person flinging the D word batters a relationship. Two using it doesn't add to the blow; it multiplies it.

Second, sometimes the D word is partly manipulation. An individual will seek personal counseling from me regarding her marriage. Because her spouse has refused to attend, she comes alone. He has been talking divorce, something she doesn't want, and further, he wants them to make the move mutually. Typically I advise her not to agree. If he is intent on breaking up, then he alone must set everything in motion. She will not cooperate in the termination of the marriage.

Sometimes one partner pushes the other toward divorce so that, in the end, the blame will be shared. "I wasn't the only one wanting to divorce; she did too." This is not grounds to provide a spouse, now or down the post-divorce road. The committed partner must not unite on so heavy a decision because the other "started it" and won't end it until the responsibility for the final act is shared. Often a marriage can survive past a nadir when one of the spouses stands strong on her values and refuses to walk side by side into a divorce.

For many who sound so sure in prodding divorce, the move itself is loaded with ambivalence. If someone has to follow through unilaterally, he may never do so. And while he tarries, the marriage is given more days to endure to better ones. To reiterate psychological mega-theme 101: Change occurs no matter what.

Third, where children live, one person talking divorce is deeply unsettling to young ears; two talking it is absolutely terrifying. Most kids desperately want to hear that one parent is trying to sustain the family, even at great personal cost. It's hard to over-state the comfort and security afforded a child who believes that at least one parent is opposing going nuclear. Studies have consistently shown that, contrary to popular "wisdom," children prefer living in a conflicted mom-and-dad family rather than in separate homes where the conflicts are less obvious. While the family is still one, they have hope.

Resistance Rationale #3: "It's not good to stay together only for the sake of the children."

Says who? This is a rationale conceived in the minds of grown-ups. I think few kids would agree with it. It springs from the notion, widespread and quite modern, that bad marriages are bad for children, and the kids would fare far better living in peace with Mom and Dad apart.

First of all, as most divorced couples will attest, peace is no guarantee after a breakup. The complications or conflicts often just take a different shape. More on that later.

Second, few conclusions in all of the social sciences have more research support than "Divorce is bad for kids young and grown." This shatters the myth that many spouses use to leave the family and pursue their own interests. It would be better for them to admit that they wish to do what they wish to do, regardless of how it affects other family members. At least that would be honest and accurate. "I'm leaving, and it'll be best for all of you," is in most cases utterly ludicrous. Such is not merely my opinion but one supported by hundreds of surveys and studies.

It is tragic beyond words, for individuals and society, that divorce is forced on so many genuinely committed to lifelong marriage. Against their will they are thrust into single parenthood with all of its stresses and distresses. Heroically they strive to give their children the best existence they can, given the realities they didn't ask for.

What if we were to ask the kids? Do they want Mom and Dad to separate? What do they think about living with two grown-ups who right now aren't getting along versus living in two different homes? After thirty years of talking to children of all ages, I know how most would answer. And even with those who would choose the breakup, most often it's from raw frustration with one or both adults, who in the kids' eyes are acting really childish, stubbornly refusing to try harder for them too. Divorce is not the option the children want; it's the one they think they have no choice but to accept.

Perhaps the most compelling rebuttal to the "for the sake of the kids" rationale is this: What better reason than the kids? Nearly every couple on the edge of divorce asserts, "I love my kids." I believe they do. I'm just not always certain what they mean by, "I love my kids." Does it imply "up to an unacceptable level of personal distress"? Is it more feeling than commitment? Is it, "I would never do anything to hurt my children, and I don't think a divorce would hurt them"?

Given the state of the marriage, no doubt they love their kids more than anybody else at the moment, including their spouse. All the more pressing then to work stronger and longer on their relationship. In their own words, the kids are their most meaningful motivation.

Of course, if one resentfully stays, changing little and counting the minutes until the youngest turns eighteen, likely the marriage will continue on its downward trajectory. Should either or both, however, resolve to persevere, if for no other reason than the children, therein could lie the impetus to survive and thrive. In time, not just for the kids but for each other, Mom and Dad may be relieved they stayed.

Resistance Rationale #4: "It's my final leverage."

At the beginning of considering this small step, I talked about addiction, specifically tolerance. Over time some drugs require higher and higher doses to produce the same results. The body adjusts to what once gave it a certain "kick" and says, "I need to be kicked harder to feel it." In short order the drug can't kick hard enough to cause any feeling. All it does is prevent the pain of withdrawal.

The *D* word kicks hard the first time. It carries all manner of "You'd better get your act together because I'm nearing my limit" implications. The blow is immediate and impactful: "This marriage is in serious trouble." No doubt that message can rattle spouses, but which ones and for how long are the unknowns.

In desperation a parent of a surly, unruly sixteen-year-old will visit my office. He is at what he's convinced is his capacity to know how to further raise this child, confessing, "I've told him, 'I've had it.' If he doesn't straighten up, he can get out."

An understandable reaction. But how realistic? Where can a sixteen-year-old go, other than to the court system or willing-to-offer-lodging friends or relatives, avenues that most parents are highly reluctant to travel? Too many questions and uncertainties lie in wait. What then does that leave?

If the threat isn't enforceable, it's ultimately empty. Soon enough the teen will realize that, if he hasn't already. Nevertheless the parent is sounding his final warning in hopes of rattling the child enough to become more cooperative.

If you don't mean the *D* word, don't say it. If you have no intention to follow through, good. The *D* word is a raised-sledge-hammer answer to a whole range of marital troubles, some slight, some heavy. It doesn't target particular problems; it pounds everything.

Using the *D* word for desired effect causes undesirable effects. First of all, as much as you might think you understand your spouse, you could miscalculate her reaction. She could be stunned, temporarily backing down from a few uncompromising attitudes. Or she could react with a surge of defensive hostility, a "Go ahead, if that's what you want." To her your reaching for this club is one more sign of how totally unreasonable you are.

Second, to borrow from the philosophers, the thought gives birth to the word gives birth to the deed. Sometimes, though, the order is different. The word gives rise to the thought. You may not be seriously leaning toward divorce, but the out-loud reiteration gives the thought more substance. A core principle of propaganda: Repeat a falsehood long and loud enough, and it becomes more believable.

One last drawback: The word could plant the thought in your spouse's head. Like you, your spouse may not yet be mulling over the final option, but as it comes out of your mouth, it lands on her ears and proceeds into her mind. After all, she concludes, if that's what you're germinating, maybe it's acceptable for her to germinate it too. Don't sow that seed.

Resistance Rationale #5: "I say it because I mean it."

It's easy to advise, "If you don't mean it, don't say it." It's much harder to advise someone who does mean it.

But even when someone does mean it, often he experiences ambivalence and anxieties, more so as the end moves nearer. The closer divorce creeps, the stronger the apprehensions. Can I be a good single parent? What about finances? How do I support my family now? Did I work at this marital mess as well as I could? Will the kids really be all right? How much will formerly good family ties, mine and his, fray or totally unravel? All of these ask the core question: "What do I mean when I say, 'I mean it'?"

Infidelity offers a dramatic illustration of "I mean it" not completely meaning "I mean it." Offended spouses often are stunned at their reaction to an affair. "I always said that if she ever cheated on me, that's it. The trust would be broken. There is no way I would live with someone I couldn't trust anymore." But to their shock they're living Psychological Truth #107: People don't always react to stressful situations as they predicted they would.

Hurt partners often find that their former rock-solid resolve to leave an unfaithful spouse—now repentant and seeking reconciliation—is wavering. So much is at stake that they will desperately search for any way to repair the damage. What once they were so certain about has become an uncertainty. They thought they meant it until the day arrived.

Returning to the observation made of those contemplating suicide, it isn't so much that they want to die; it's that they don't want to live, not in their current emotional state anyway. Those living in what seems to be the death throes of a long-worsening marriage may not want divorce with all its ramifications. But neither do they want to live so maritally miserably. In their minds divorce would be leaving a bad scene for a better one or, at a minimum, a less bad one.

To which I ask, "How do you *know* you are leaving a bad scene for a better one? Given all the changes, unpredictability, stresses, and added demands, can you *really* be certain where you're heading?" To be sure, the daily companion, frustration, may lessen, bringing some peace. The familiar struggles are over. But what unfamiliar struggles lie ahead?

If one is a parent, the questions multiply. How will I be able to guide my children's upbringing and morals when they're with their mom? Am I prepared to surrender a portion of my supervision? What about romantic interests that enter my ex-spouse's life and thus my children's? Will he remarry? Will there be step-siblings? What will they be like? Mature? Pleasant? Worldly? Nasty? Abusive? Will the kids increasingly prefer to live with Disney Parent? Will I need to work more and harder to support the family, leaving less time for the stuff of parenthood? What directions—morally, socially, geographically—will my ex-spouse's life take, and how will all of that reverberate on my family, the original and any new one?

A survey asked individuals five years post-divorce, "Are you more content than you were in your marriage?" Fifty percent admitted to being as unhappy, or more so, now than then.[1] Powerful evidence that what we think we're "trading up" for may not turn out to be such a good personal bargain.

It must be repeated: Many have divorce pressed upon them against their will by an uncommitted spouse or a seriously disturbed one. Others have to separate for reasons of safety or critical threats to the family's well-being. Still, more often than not, one or both partners are simply dissatisfied with aspects of the relationship. And here is where healing is still quite possible.

If you think you mean divorce when you say it, please think longer and harder about what it could mean. You may not necessarily be moving from a bad existence to a good one. You could just as likely (survey says, 50–50) be moving from a known bad—with potential for better—to an unknown bad.

D *Word Scenario*

Therapist: We enter the dialogue twenty-eight minutes in progress. Most D-word eruptions don't prompt arguments. They are byproducts when exchanges hit a certain temperature.

Husband: If I'm so hard to live with, then why do you want to even keep living with me?

Therapist: Not always does someone admit to thinking divorce. Sometimes the desire is projected upon the other. "I'm not saying I want this, but maybe you do."

Wife: What are you saying? You really think I want to end this marriage?

Husband: It sure seems like it. I don't seem to be able to do anything right in your eyes anymore.

Therapist: Often the D thought comes on the tail of, "I've tried everything with you. There's nothing left."

Wife: I know we've had our trouble—lots of it—but let's not start talking of breaking apart. I don't want that. If we're going to battle, let's not start there.

Therapist: If one spouse immediately and definitely denies that divorce is in his or her mind, it can deflect the other's charge.

Husband: I don't want that either. But sometimes it looks to me like that's where we're headed.

Therapist: After initially projecting the desire onto the other, Husband acknowledges that it came first to his mind. Though not obvious, he may be saying, "Reassure me that you're not thinking that." Sometimes the D word is used to probe, to say, "I don't want it if you don't."

Wife: That's not where I'm headed. Can't we disagree without that kind of talk? That doesn't do any good for either of us.

Therapist: If one spouse talks divorce more, the reluctant one needs to keep squelching the idea. Two people hinting separation has a synergistic effect: Each reinforces the other. Any wrong-way momentum is slowed when only one person does the pushing.

Husband: Well, maybe you ought to think a little harder about the way you treat me, because I have a limit on what I'm willing to take.

Wife: If I don't treat you right, it's not because I want out or even want to quit trying.

Therapist: Wife has admirably avoided getting caught up in the side issues of the exchange. She keeps reiterating, in so many words, "I know we've got our problems, but I'm not at all looking at splitting as a solution." A good message to repeat, especially during a recurrent theme of, "Divorce is an option."

The Last Word

Once the divorce door is cracked open, or merely stepped toward, a temptation gains a foothold. "I can escape if life doesn't improve." The impulses are antagonistic. Talking and thinking divorce deadens the desire to talk and think better marriage. There is an ever present out.

On the other hand, if from my mind and mouth I have eliminated the D word, I have little choice but to work harder within my marriage. With divorce not an answer, my drive to repair what is broken will be more urgent.

What if the option has been spoken, repeatedly? It's never too late to take back bad words. Say you're sorry. Approach your spouse during a calm, confessing that you were speaking out of emotion and exasperation. You do not want what the word represents, and you will work hard never to say it again, no matter how upset you might get.

Admitting and regretting are salutary. They can start to heal those hurts generating the *D* word.

These first six small steps are meant to lessen verbal strife. Disrespect, in whatever form, corrodes a relationship. It eats away at civility and good will. Nasty words give the most minor of disagreements the potential to become major trouble. That is why the emphasis has been first placed on simple strategies to ease discord while promoting peace.

Next we will take some small steps toward a warmer relationship overall.

| *Use Your Manners* |

Parents expend loads of energy teaching manners. Simple courtesy is among the earliest and most emphasized of social skills. My guess is that the typical parent instructs, demonstrates, and cajoles the typical child thousands of times prior to first grade. Should thousands sound like an overstatement, consider that if a parent attends to manners three times per day, in one year he exceeds the one-thousand mark.

Most parents rely upon the standards: "What do you say?" "How do you ask nicely?" "Say, 'Excuse me.'" "What's the magic word?" The drill is relentlessly repetitive, exhausting even, especially given that we are not shaping morals and character—the broader stuff of good personhood—though one could reasonably argue that simple courtesy does birth more mature virtues.

Why such emphasis on politeness? Because manners are more than mutually agreed upon rules of etiquette—they are a means of offering dignity. They communicate, "I will treat you with social grace because I think you deserve it." Good manners speak well, not only of oneself but also of the person to whom they're addressed.

Most people extrapolate from courtesy, rightly or wrongly, a host of admirable attributes—kindness, respect, maturity. And they reciprocate. Mannerly youngsters get affection, compliments, and extra cookies from the server. In short, manners benefit both giver and recipient.

At one time my ten children were all aged twelve and under. I remember asking my wife if she minded my moving into the garage for a few years. She minded.

As other parents do, we began focusing on politeness early, inside and outside the house. The process left both of us hoarse. When without prompting the kids did display good manners in public—about 10 to 12 percent of the time—other adults reacted positively. Variations of "What nice kids" or "Such good manners" or "Isn't she sweet?" were sent our way and the kids'.

Part of me—the psychologist part—fought the urge to respond, "Thanks, but you really don't know if she's sweet or not. Don't survey her brothers." Part of me—the parent part—swelled with the accolades, and I asked the server for an extra cookie for myself too.

It's easy to become loose with manners as kids get older. In part we figure, "He's got the idea now" and needs no reminding. In part we get sloppier overall in our parenting. That's been true for me. With Andrew, our first child, I required an automatic "Please" and "Thank you" to get and keep anything. With Lizzy, our youngest, I punished Andrew for not saying "Please" for her.

Whatever the reason, if not reinforced, manners tend toward decay. Many a fourteen-year-old doesn't display the same level of courtesy displayed by the typical five-year-old. To the young ones manners still have a feel of novelty. With age a sort of social inertia sets in. Keeping little words of gratitude and kindness to oneself becomes the path of least resistance.

Law of Manners #101 states, "The warmer the relationship between two people, the more critical are manners." Law of Manners #102 states, "The colder the relationship between two people, the more critical are manners."

Sadly, in warm and cold marriages alike, manners all too easily are neglected or jettisoned altogether. In stronger marriages spouses can drift into a laziness born of comfort. "She knows how I feel; I don't see the need to always be telling her that she's special." The trend toward less courtesy is not a reflection of fewer feelings but more of apathy. It just seems normal. Though what is normal is not necessarily what is good.

In weaker marriages a lack of good manners is a byproduct of a lack of good will. "I am not moved to be polite because I am not moved to be nice." Or, "We have so many troubles, poor manners isn't even in our top ten."

Whatever the temperature of your marriage, most likely you and your spouse have room for a little added social grace. Likeable people become more likeable when treated with courtesy. Unlikeable people become a little less unlikeable.

Having no manners, or bad ones, does more than convey apathy or disrespect. It can breed resentment. If I routinely use more courtesy with others than with my own spouse, and she knows it, the message is loud: "I work harder at being pleasant to anyone—pastor, plumber, or persnickety people—than I do to you." Placing a spouse at the lower end of one's manners list can bruise any relationship.

Small step #7 may be the smallest step. Say, "Please," "Thank you," "Excuse me." A grand total of five words, and all but one, one syllable. Simple to pronounce. Most easily added to any other group of words.

Like a spice, manners can add life to something bland. Unlike spices, they are hard to overuse. The more, the better. And you needn't be a preschooler to receive in return the benefits: gratitude, compliments, softness, manners.

Resistance Rationale #1: "I'm not a little kid."

Possibly not. But who among us couldn't take a few lessons from what seems to come naturally to little kids—a willingness to forgive, an eagerness to please, a readiness to use manners? Which traits does a parent strive to instill in her child only for a childhood? Who instructs, "Tell the truth until you're eighteen"; "Don't punch your brother until you're both adults"; "Say 'Please' and 'Thank you' until you get a job." If valuable for a childhood, a quality is valuable for a lifetime. If manners are desirable habits for the young, so should they be for the older, even more so.

Have you ever treated another—boss, best friend, mother-in-law—with consistent courtesy and endured, "OK, can you ease off some on this manners thing? The first fifty or so times it was nice, but it's getting old. Our relationship is mature enough now that these little pleasantries aren't necessary anymore."?

Some might object, "I know how to use manners. I'm not a child who needs to be reminded." Yes and no. As an adult, if manners are second nature to you, you need no prompting. You internalized the concept long ago. But if you "learned" your manners young yet in the years since have let the learning lapse, particularly with your spouse, a little nudge could help rejuvenate your old childhood habit.

"I'm not a little kid" is true, in the literal sense. Yet this Resistance Rationale can lurk in a more subtle guise. That is, one may not actually fear coming across childlike if his manners are too good, but he could fear being vulnerable, putting himself into what some psychologists have labeled a "one down" position. What kind of reaction might he receive by talking pleasantly? Suspicion? Rejection? A blank look? "I'm trying to be nice, and I'm being dismissed. I'm gingerly reaching out, and she's slapping my hand."

While an adult's manners don't evoke the "Isn't she sweet?" given a child, courtesy at any age can soften, if not another's heart, his demeanor. Most have learned the hard way that politeness evokes far more genuine cooperation from a clerk or server than assertive demanding. Should your spouse perceive your winning words as odd sounding or overdone, be patient. In time he should come to hear you as pretty mature, maybe more so than he, in the social graces anyway. (I did say "maybe.")

Resistance Rationale #2: "I don't have any desire to use manners."

This resistance made itself heard with the very first small step, "Say, I'm sorry." In fact, it could be listed as the first resistance to any small step. In fact, it could be the first resistance to nearly any good behavior. In fact, if left unchallenged, it could pretty much paralyze counseling. In fact, it could pretty much paralyze most any self-improvement.

At some level, "I don't feel like it" is the resistance underlying most other resistances. And we'll give it its own space near the end of this book. For now let's analyze the desire that might or might not partner with manners.

Most people expect some apologetic feelings—regret, remorse, guilt—to accompany a sincere apology. They can think that to offer an "I'm sorry" when one is not would be misleading if not downright deceptive. Genuine words of repentance, they believe, need genuine feelings to give them full meaning. Though again, as we discussed in our small step #1, sometimes the words alone can begin the healing.

Words of courtesy don't demand the same linkage between the act and the emotion. "Please hand me the coffee" doesn't call for some minimum level of warmth to be legitimate. It can stand on its own. Likewise, "Thank you" (for the coffee) is a simple sign of appreciation. It needn't be accompanied by some deep-felt sense of gratitude.

Much proper conduct would never advance if one had to feel the urge before moving with it. A bad habit, by repetition, becomes second nature. Replacing it with a good habit is a passage, one that can sit uneasy for a while. The first tentative courtesies may come with few positive impulses, while their antagonist —neglect of courtesy—has been the resident style. It will continue to dominate until pushed out.

With or without feelings, manners are good. With practice the motivation to speak courtesies will grow, for anyone in earshot. Please think about this. Thanks.

Resistance Rationale #3: "I've tried to be nice; it doesn't work."
Good conduct is its own reward. The results may not be what were desired. No matter. The best of motivations is selfless: This is what I ought to do.

As a men's softball team coach, I've faced the following game situation. It's the bottom of the last inning. My team is ahead by one run. The opposing team is batting with two outs and has runners on second and third base. Their best hitter is coming to bat.

Standard coaching strategy would be to deliberately walk the batter, putting him on first base, bringing a weaker hitter to the plate as well as setting up a "force," an easier way to get an out. To condense all this ball jargon, if one is trying to win the game, this is the move to make. So I make it. Subsequently their next batter hits a single, and two runs score. We lose.

Did I make a poor coaching decision? No. Though we didn't win, it was the smart call.

Using an example closer to home, so to speak, families often clash over how to morally address a problem or crisis. If one side "wins," the other might counter with, "We'll see if you did the right thing by how it turns out." How it turns out is no way to judge the "right thing." If something is right, it is right, regardless of its results.

In therapy a wife will disclose, "The only time he's affectionate with me is when he wants to go further physically." I might then advise hubby to spontaneously hug and kiss a little more, with no other motive. Next session he'll report that he gave fifteen hugs and twelve kisses but mostly encountered, "Don't. You're sweaty," or, "That doesn't feel good," or, "Not right now. I'm washing my face." His first hesitant gestures at no-expectations affection were unsuccessful, so he abandoned them indefinitely.

From parents I regularly hear the lament, "I've tried every kind of discipline with this child. Nothing works. Finally I got so frustrated, I sent him next door to run an errand and moved away while he was gone."

All right, my exaggeration is for effect. Typically along the way, the parents had used several good approaches. They didn't give them enough time, mistakenly assuming that if were they on the right track, home life would be looking noticeably better. One discipline rule of thumb: For every one year the trouble has been present, stick with your approach for one month. This is an even better rule, I believe, for relationships.

Anything worth doing is worth doing for a while. And three weeks, or three months, even three years, may not be "a while" when measured against the length of its antithetical habit. Your first twenty-two *thank-you*s may beget only two *you're welcome*s. But four months from now, you might receive ten for your twenty-two, a fivefold improvement. Whatever the final ratio, your goal is to get beyond zero to zero.

Resistance Rationale #4: "I don't always use manners, but I ask nicely."

"Can you iron these pants for me?" is nicer than, "Iron these pants for me," which is nicer than, "You call these ironed?" and is way nicer than, "My mother really knew the right way to iron pants." (Men, best keep this last opinion to yourself. Otherwise from here forward you or your mother may have to iron all your pants.)

The nicest way to ask is, "When you have time, would you please iron these pants? Thank you." Mannerly words just sound better.

Why would parents work so diligently to reinforce a child's use of particular words? Why not just instruct, "It doesn't matter what you say, as long as you say it pleasantly"? Because some words more than others signal social grace. A gentle tone and phrasing, to be sure, provide a foundation. Courtesy, however, is completed through using identifiable mannerly words.

My seventeen-year-old son, Sam, accuses me of "hinting." Instead of talking straight, I imply. For example, calling home I'll ask, "Is Mom there?"

Briskly, Sammy answers, "Yes," and hangs up. Not really—he knows better, I think—but he does ask, "Do you want to talk to her?"

My demeanor is agreeable, but my phone etiquette could be clearer. "Hi, Sammy. May I please talk to Mom?"

In fact, that's how I instruct the kids to ask. Pleasant, mannerly, with no hinting. Of course, if Sammy ever would hang up on me, I'd be forced to call back and employ some definite fatherly hinting: "Sam, do you think what you just did was in your best interests?"

One form of learning is called classical conditioning. Does the name Pavlov ring a bell? Classical conditioning involves pairing a neutral event with a meaningful event—for example, the ringing of a bell with the dispensing of food to a hungry dog. With repetition the sound of the bell by itself stimulates the reaction that the food alone once did—salivation and heading toward the food dispenser.

Manners are a linguistic example of classical conditioning. Certain words are paired with pleasantness so many times across so many situations that in themselves they carry social power. Am I hinting that your spouse has the temperament of a hungry dog? Not always, I'd guess. But the principles of classical conditioning apply both to dogs and humans. Use them to maximum benefit.

Resistance Rationale #5: "It sounds forced, even unnatural."

One subtle challenge to learning a new language is that merely changing a phrase's tone can radically change its meaning. Depending on the inflection, "Thanks a lot" can say, "I don't appreciate that one bit." "Oh, please" can convey, "Don't give me that." And comedian Steve Martin's old signature line,

"Well, *excuuuse* me," wasn't seeking permission; it declared, "Pardon me for living." Tricky stuff, this linguistics.

No question, if not accompanied by the right tone, "manners" can be insults. Rather than being vehicles for respect, they can deliver disrespect: disdain, disgust, or disappointment. Their only resemblance to genuine politeness lies in their spelling.

To make manners sound more natural, cease using them in any other way. No sarcasm. No snide commentary. No put-downs. The quicker the transition from misuse to good use, the more quickly they'll sound genuine. You don't want another thinking, "You've used these same words before. I know what they mean."

Then, too, don't assume your spouse can read your inside by your outside. Many surveys confirm that others can't easily gauge how someone is feeling by how she looks. For instance, those who experience near paralyzing anxiety in social situations believe others can see how distressed they are. Not so. Anxiety is primarily an internal state; it is not readily obvious to others.

A parallel can be drawn to manners. Your words, if not paired with gritted teeth and bulging eyes, will sound more real than they might feel. Likely your spouse will hear them so too, especially if that spouse is a husband. That's not sexist; that's reality. As a group guys are not as sensitive to subtle social cues as are women. Just ask my ten-year-old daughter or my twenty-year-old son.

Finally, as can't be said enough, any kind of novel behavior can seem foreign. Humans rapidly grow comfortable with predictability. Something that breaks the pattern can sound and feel strange or strained. Almost all natural behavior, however, was once new—unnatural, if you will. Only with ongoing presence does it evolve into the routine and familiar. So it is with courtesy. Eventually the new verbal you will become the authentic verbal you.

Manners Scenario

Wife: Your daughter Melissa needs to be driven to soccer practice.

Therapist: Sometimes one can forgo manners by making a direct statement: "The dishes need to be washed." Note also Mom's not-so-subtle reminder to Dad that it is his *daughter requiring transportation.*

Husband: When does she have to leave? I took her yesterday. Can't you take her?

Wife: Yes, you took her yesterday. But I took her the three days before that. Besides, I have things to do here. It won't take you that long. Please.

Therapist: Please changes the direction of the interchange, from argument to asking. Still, if Dad is determined to balk, a whole bunch of pleases *may not budge his bottom from the La-Z-Boy. Mom, though, is playing the odds. Which message has the better chance of success? "You're just lazy," or "Please consider this"?*

Wife: I'd really appreciate it if you would.

Therapist: Wife is doubling her manners: an outright please *and a variant of* thank-you. *She's not groveling but is appealing to Husband's tentative sense of teamwork.*

Husband: Where is she? Is she ready to go now?

Wife: I'll get her for you.

Therapist: Whether it was Mom's second attempt at courtesy or not, Dad acquiesced.

Manners, of course, don't guarantee cooperation. In the realm of human communication, not too much does. The likelihood of pleasant compliance, however, rises with each courteous discourse.

Wife (as husband is slouching out the door with Melissa): Thank you.

Husband: That's OK.

Therapist: In husband-speak, "That's OK" is a weak paraphrase of "You're welcome." Getting reciprocal politeness sometimes takes a few intermediate steps.

The Last Word

Some advice is too vague to be of much help. To exhort a spouse to be nice to her mate may be wise counsel, but it's not very practical. What exactly does *nice* mean? A therapist urging a depressed patient to "cheer up" or an upset one to "relax" may well know that's needed. But just how does one take concrete steps to cheer up or relax?

Manners are a concrete first step toward being nicer. They provide a working formula of sorts. The words are specific, can readily accompany most communication, and kindle good will. Manners are one little means to a broader end: a nicer relationship.

| *Protect* |

If you're a father, this step is yours to initiate. If you're a mother, you'll be the first to reap the benefits, but soon they'll follow to your husband and children. If your husband isn't inclined to read these kinds of books, and he won't sit quietly by long enough for you to read to him, you could copy and strategically place this chapter where he regularly alights—near the remote or the toilet.

In counseling and in conversation, I'm hearing a similar refrain from more women: They are the lead authorities in their homes. They do most of the disciplining, enforce the bulk of the rules, and set the higher expectations for the kids. Variously they refer to the men as Disney Dad, Mr. Oblivious, Mr. Good-time-nice-guy. Some husbands offer defenses like, "Honey, I was that way when I was a kid, and I think I turned out all right." Whereupon the women bite their lips to keep from retorting, "Let's gather the relatives and vote."

Many dads are comfortable with this arrangement. While Mom does the lioness's share of the discipline, they hang back, letting her take the brunt of the kids' resistance or, worse yet, undercutting her. Perhaps they disagree with her decision or style or are aiming to be peacemakers. Whatever the intent, this pattern can widen a parental rift and, with it, a marital one.

Men, would you passively stand by as another adult verbally mistreated your wife? Particularly if you yourself are respectful toward her? Even if that adult is your mother? Would it not be reasonable then for you to stand up to your kids and defend your wife? Envision the scene.

Your wife and child are locked in a bicker fest. You're tempted to remain buried in the recliner, all the while thinking, "If I close my eyes, I can't tell which one is the twelve-year-old." Resist that temptation. Get up. Get in there. Get involved. In a word, protect.

"That's not only your mom you're talking to that way; that's my wife. Go to your room. I'm going to see what she wants me to do about this (OK, so the first few times you're nervous about standing on your own), and then I'm going to do more."

Your goal? Step in and stop that child from harassing your wife. Don't use feeble words like, "Is that how you talk to your mother?" or, "You watch your mouth, young man," or the really wimpy, "Don't make me come in there." Take action. Not only will you enhance your image as a man, but you will respect hers as a woman, several ways.

First, your wife is facing a resistant or difficult youngster. Her demeanor is fast moving toward exasperation, if not already there. Your presence will soothe some of the agitation.

Second, she's likely feeling besieged. She's going head-to-head with this child, or children, alone. She is either fatigued or out-numbered. You shift the balance back into her favor, where it belongs.

Third, even if your wife has grown accustomed to contending with childish resistance by herself, she may still wonder, "Where is he?" She knows you're hearing the melee—how could you not?—and she's hoping that this time backup is coming. You won't disappoint.

Your action will ring loud: "I value you enough to defend you. I will protect something that means much to you, your motherhood."

Resistance Rationale #1: "I've never done anything like this before."

From birth forward every single thing we do begins as a "never before" behavior. The most long-standing habit was once the first time. Granted, much conduct is just a variation on some core traits, but even the variations were once brand new.

"I've never done this before" can mean a number of things. One, "I've never tried this before"—written a book, played chess, changed a diaper, cliff dived. The activity is novel, but it's not a contradiction of my personality. New pursuits don't necessarily challenge one's stable self-perception.

Two, "This conduct is out of character for me. It's not my way." Think, for instance, "I'm sorry. I was wrong. Can I do anything to help you? I'll carry that; it looks heavy. You go rest; I'll finish up in here."

Three, "I've engaged in this pattern sporadically. It's nothing I do with any consistency."

Four, "I have a strong tendency to act in the opposite direction. My prevailing habit is so ingrained as to seriously interfere with my behaving otherwise."

Meanings three and four would seem most relevant to this particular resistance rationale. Let's assume you would rather cliff dive than leap into a swirling parent-child maelstrom. In the past you have jumped in only when hurricane volume has been reached.

Feeling out of place your first few ventures into the cross-currents is understandable. The waters are unfamiliar. What turbulence will you encounter? Are you in over your head? Your wife also could wonder, "Who are you? What have you done with my husband?"

Even your child(ren) may not know what to think. They're accustomed to your watching from a distance. They've come to interpret your inaction as tacit approval of their action. Are you about to switch sides?

No matter who reacts how, your first-time immersion will be the first time only once. After that each succeeding Dad presence will slowly alter everybody's perceptions, yours included. Repetition is how the unexpected becomes routine.

Sir Isaac Newton discovered the scientific law of inertia. In part it declared, "A body at rest will remain at rest unless acted upon by an outside force." To humanize this law, a body (Dad's) will remain at rest (on the couch) unless acted upon by an outside force (Mom's call for help, an ear-splitting child noise, the dog's agitated howling).

The parallel to physics is not perfect, however. For us men the force is not always outside. It is inside, in the mind. Overcoming a reluctance to move—our psychological inertia—involves an internal tug-of-war. We must be convinced that activity is better than passivity. If what I hear from many beleaguered moms is any indication, it is.

The law of inertia also states, "A body in motion tends to stay in motion unless acted upon by an outside force." Once you start to move in defense of your wife, the behavioral momentum will grow. The habit will become more who you are rather than "Who are you?"

Resistance Rationale #2: "I don't know how she'll react."

Neither do I. Not for certain anyway. You could encounter a range of reactions.

One, shock. Your wife may wonder what alien life form has penetrated her husband's mind and for how long. Still, this doesn't mean she'll refuse your help. Surprise doesn't mean rejection.

Two, mistrust. She's wary of your motive. She interprets your involvement as questioning her discipline and, by extension, her motherhood. Reassure her that, one, in no way are you implying anything is wrong with her parenting, and two, you are there to support. You may, in fact, see her style as fueling the trouble, but keep that observation to yourself. You're already facing one upset person, the child; don't add a second.

Ask your wife, "What can I do to help you here?" That should release some of the steam from the scene. Should she remain resistant, consider a strategic retreat. You'll have more opportunities to reenter, as long as kids are kids and parents are parents.

A third reaction is rejection. In her eyes you are too strict, overbearing, or authoritative, and you would just make the situation worse. Here I'd like to address the women. If in fact your husband's discipline is overdone, temper it if possible, advising that, despite how it sounds, you do have things under control.

On the other hand, before concluding that he's being heavy-handed, ask yourself, "Is he firmer, so he seems 'meaner'? Does he use fewer words, thereby sounding less 'flexible'? Is he a stronger presence, so he exudes more authority?" Put simply, does he discipline unlike you?

Studies say that overall men and women do discipline differently, especially with young kids. As a group men are less verbal and more action inclined, and because of size and voice, they can come across as more intimidating. None of this is bad in itself. It is guy style. Is Dad being too tough, or is he just manlier than Mom?

Sometimes in therapy a wife will tell me she's uneasy with the way her husband disciplines. It's too direct, too strong. While she may readily acknowledge that he is a loving father who would never hurt his children, she'd like him to be softer. I ask, "Do you mean more motherlike?" If her answer is yes, I may suggest, "Let Dad have his own personal style. Allow him to discipline as a man, in the healthiest sense of the word."

Back to the men now. When you do intervene, don't roar in like a wounded bear. Be quiet and steady, not loud and threatening. Come to discipline, not dominate. The more calmly self-confident you are, the more confidence your wife will have in you.

The reaction you are most likely to receive? Warm welcome. At marriage conferences, after exhorting the husbands to "protect," I watch wives' body language, subtle and not so. Head nods, knowing grins, female elbows probing male ribs—all unspoken "You should do more of that," and "I'd be real pleased if you did." Other wives give their husbands an arm hug or squeeze, meaning, "You do that. Thank you." Most all the wives are saying the same thing, "I want your presence."

Resistance Rationale #3: "She doesn't like the way I discipline." We answered this somewhat with the last Resistance Rationale. Let's elaborate.

The rule rather than the exception is that a mother and father, however one in their parenting goals, are not always one in discipline. No two histories, personalities, emotional profiles, or tolerance levels are identical. Hence no two discipline approaches are identical. Each spouse brings his or her own personality to the child-rearing front. The ideal is that each one's strengths compensate some for the other's weaknesses.

When spouses differ, it is as often over style as over substance. For example, both want respectful children; on that they converge. Where they diverge is in their practice. Dad sees Mom as excusing of tone and attitude he would prohibit. Mom thinks Dad lets disrespect multiply before he acts, and then he overreacts. The criticisms center more on the other's methods rather than standards.

Many mothers tell me they'd like more discipline support, but they're nervous about the way it comes packaged. So rather than inviting another contentious voice into an already contentious situation, they accept the lesser of two unpleasant options and discipline solo.

If your spouse is upset by your manner of discipline, does she have a point? Do you stay away from the fray until it gets too loud for your liking? Or until you're highly agitated from hearing the back and forth escalate? Or until it interferes with the final two minutes of a tied football game?

In other words, do you ignore, ignore, tolerate, tolerate, erupt? And is it the eruption that most distresses your wife? If you intervened sooner, before the "I've had enough" stage, would you be more composed? Could you act more evenhandedly, letting your consequences do your talking? In my experience very few moms truly object to an in-control, take-control dad, especially one who's defending them.

Should your disagreements stem from differing standards, you'd be wise to exercise caution, restraint even, in choosing when and where to protect. Proceed slowly, being vigilant for those situations noticeably unpleasant for your wife. When you sense her getting frustrated or desperate, that may be your signal to insert yourself into the scene. She needs an ally, however "imperfect" she thinks him. Make your demeanor say, "I'm here to stand with my wife and your mother," as opposed to, "You're in double the trouble now, Kid, because I had to get involved."

Once more, to be better welcomed, keep your discipline, discipline. Don't clutter it up with excessive words and volume. You're there to act, not yak. Manly strength is not measured by decibels and threats; it is measured by calm confidence.

Resistance Rationale #4: "My wife needs to establish her own authority."

You are not usurping your wife's authority; you are doubling it. You're telling the kids, "Mom and I are a team." Two in one.

Does the better player on a tennis doubles team subtract from his partner's game or add to it? Does the top hitter on a baseball team make his team better or worse by his talent? Does his skill hinder his teammates from reaching their personal best? The analogies are not perfect, but one spouse's strong discipline can make the other's better by its presence. It can carry both to the common goal—great kids.

Maybe you're thinking that, in an ideal world, your wife would adroitly handle every challenge with ever-patient, confident consistency. Most if not all conflicts would never reach your ears, as she would quickly and quietly defuse them. Alas, such a scenario lives only in parenting book examples. Or in the mind of your mother, who regales your wife at every chance with how competently she raised you. In the real-life world of parents and kids, inconsistent and incomplete authority is the norm, as it is inextricably bound up with being human.

If your wife is spinning her wheels during a child-driven ruckus, you could park in another room, allowing her to make clear her authority. If that doesn't happen, the greater will be her frustration, and the longer it will linger. And don't assume that, because you remained neutral, you'll be untouched by it all. Someone might be a bit upset that you sat out the round.

Of course, you're not defenseless: "Honey, I was just waiting for you to establish your own authority. You don't need me butting in. By the way, have you seen the remote and the chip dip?"

Your "butting in" actually helps your wife establish her authority.

- First, it pulls the plug on the conflict. The longer a parent resides verbally at a child's level, the more authority he or she loses. The sooner you support your spouse, the sooner parental authority stabilizes.
- Second, you provide a model. Although she may not naturally do things your way, your wife could observe your way, over time incorporating some of your better techniques into her own approach. When you're not there to demonstrate your discipline superiority but to share the discipline load, you're far better received.

Husbands will maintain, "She causes her own frustration. She overtalks, overreasons, overnegotiates."

Here we must distinguish between authority and method. Even if Mom's discipline method could use some doctoring, she still has authority. She may assert it poorly, but by virtue of her motherhood, she has a rightful claim to it.

Suppose you're sitting in a courtroom due to a traffic violation. Prior to your case you've listened to the magistrate belittle defendants and overall display a hostile demeanor. Comes your turn, you offer the argument, "Judge, I don't think you've earned any right to fine me. Your judicial decorum stinks. When you can act appropriate, reschedule my case."

If you have no lawyer, get one quick. His or her approach to the bench will almost certainly begin with, "Your Honor, my client would like to offer a sincere apology. Obviously he was confused about your statutory status. We acknowledge your full right to adjudicate matters according to your duly established authority."

If your spouse has been struggling with discipline for years, when is it finally time to lend a discipline hand? Mothers and fathers are unequal coequals in parenting. One might be the warmer and more complimenting; the other might be more clear-cut in expectations. One's discipline speed limit may be a school zone's; the other's is the autobahn's. Partners are there to complement each other, offering what the other might lack.

I've played softball for over three decades. In my younger days I was an outfielder. Now I pitch, as my legs, eyes, and arm no longer cooperate with my head. To keep the team winning, I recruit younger, faster players. When a twenty-three-year-old makes a diving catch I can only duplicate now in my dreams, I am grateful. What I lack in athletic ability, he possesses. I can still throw strikes. He can run down fly balls. We are a team.

Your wife's authority won't be diminished by you asserting yours, especially when it's done in her service.

Protection Scenario

Mom: Well, Melissa, since you asked, I can think of about six reasons why I'm not allowing you to go to the mall and meet with girls I don't even know.

Melissa: Mom, get a clue. You don't even know what you're talking about.

Dad (from another room): You'd better control your mouth, young lady.

Therapist: Dad did orient toward the disrespect, but he made no move. He flung a warning, but the fact is Melissa's mouth already is not being controlled.

Further, the farther away, the less authority one has. Dad can't establish a protective presence if he's not present.

Melissa: I'm fifteen. My friends have been meeting people at the mall for years. None of them agree with you at all.

Mom: That's them, and you're you. And because you're only fifteen is one reason you're not allowed to go.

Melissa: See, this is why I don't even try to talk to you. You already have your mind made up because you're always the boss.

Mom: Why don't you ask Dad? See what he says.

Therapist: Mom is showing little awareness of Melissa's disrespect. Still, she's reaching for spousal help. She is not passively waiting for Dad to intervene. She must know he'll agree with her; otherwise she wouldn't risk being undercut.

Melissa: Yeah, right. He'll just agree with you because he has to.

Dad (rousing himself to enter the action): What's going on in here?

Therapist: Bad entrance. First of all, "What's going on in here?" is already obvious. Melissa is disagreeably disagreeing with her mother's reasonable decision. Second, the question can come across as "holding court." That is, Dad is coming in to judge the nature of the problem and either declare a compromise or, worse, parcel out blame.

Two facts are clear in this case. One, Mom has full right to make determinations for Melissa's well-being. Two, Melissa is being downright surly about that. Let's give Dad a second entrance.

Dad (entering the room of the altercation): Melissa, I don't like at all what I'm hearing from you. You seem to have forgotten that's your mom you're talking to. Not only are you not allowed to go, but this discussion is over, and you are in your room. This is not just your mom's decision; it is mine, too.

Therapist: Dad and Mom have allowed several disdainful comebacks. Only when Dad hits his emotional trip switch does he act. Nevertheless, he does recover. In laying out his consequences, Dad couples himself to Mom's ruling, thus dividing the target for any more of Melissa's nastiness.

Melissa (leaving the room): Whatever. You always do what she wants anyway.

Dad: Well, now you've just earned your room for the rest of the night. And tomorrow Mom and I both will decide what to do about your attitude. Good night.

(Turning to wife): Are you OK? She was pretty snotty. Next time she argues with you like that and I'm around, call me in right off. Sometimes I'm just oblivious.

Therapist: Nice ending on Dad's part. Not only is he concerned for his wife's likely battered feelings, but he's doing a little humble self-introspection. On a protection scale of one to ten, his overall score is about a seven. If he follows through tomorrow, 7.9.

The Last Word

Protect your wife. You'll be doing much more than momentarily shielding her from a resistant or rude child. You will protect her person, her dignity as a mother. Others in your family will benefit, too.

By teaching your children respect, you will be protecting them from the world's teaching, which would otherwise hit them with much harder lessons later in life.

You yourself will benefit. No longer are you a bystander who lets Mom do most of the family tough stuff. You will strengthen the family's image of you as the man of the house. Protect, and in the end the person most protected may be you.

| *Make a List* |

Praise, the heart of good relationships. Everyone—from the youngest child to the oldest psychologist—instinctively understands the value of giving and receiving personal accolades. The most faultfinding spouses will admit, however reluctantly, that a few compliments sprinkled about would elevate the environment.

None of this is my prelude to steering you to a goal of five compliments per day or one per month, whichever is more reachable. First, that would be redundant with the million or so books and articles, give or take a few hundred thousand, already advising that. Second, as a therapist I see the resistance to giving kudos in strained relationships, some of which we'll answer shortly.

The universe is governed by the law of entropy. It states that everything tends toward decay. Iron rusts, our bodies age, the sun will eventually burn out. Though pertaining to the physical world, the law of entropy has relevance to some human behavior as well.

Few aspects of a relationship are as prone to decay as the voicing of uplifting words. Comfortable marriages can become so comfortable that conscious efforts at complimenting are allowed to grow flaccid. "He knows how I feel about him. I don't need to keep saying it." Or, "She sees by my actions what I think." She'll see it only if those actions are consistent and not mixed in their messages.

Little affirmation attends poorer marriages because ill will crowds out the willingness to give any kind of credit. Sadly, the prevailing attitude often is "Until you start being easier to live with, I'm not about to massage your ego." In essence, "I don't think you deserve compliments, even if they're true."

A tongue-in-cheek commentary on marriage goes as follows. During the first year of marriage, each time a husband and wife share physical intimacy, they are to place one marble in a jar. After the first year, for each marital union they are to remove one marble from that jar. The jar will never be empty. A bit of an exaggeration perhaps, but holding a kernel of truth: We are more animated—thereby we try harder—in the first stages of knowing someone.

So it seems with compliments. As a rule their number early on supersedes if not dwarfs their number over later years, even in praiseworthy marriages. To repeat, I am not about to press you to scour for times and places to extend positive remarks. If you're so moved, great; I compliment you. The smallest rise in spontaneous verbal kindness can tone down the meaner stuff.

"Make a List" is what I suggest. That means, write down what you admire, appreciate, and like about your spouse. Some of you might demur that this step goes beyond writing to straining. I suppose it could be somewhat of a mental workout. And we all know the soreness that comes if one hasn't exercised in a while.

Why the "write and say"? Why not just a "think and say"? Because writing both expands and focuses one's thoughts at the same time. It provides a structure for gathering together some positives, many long ignored or long unspoken. It coaxes more to come to mind.

I may be convinced that I've got a marriage book living in my head. All I need to do is translate it to paper. So I think until I start to write. Then, somewhere between my head and the paper, I discover other ideas, which were probably in me in some vague form but needed to be shaped by actual language. The written word is a good medium for taking something from mind to reality.

Your list has no maximum length; it'd better have a minimum. Otherwise it becomes the proverbial backhanded compliment. Its skimpiness will speak louder than its few pieces of flattery, no matter how sweet each might be.

What do you do with your list? Find a good time and place to share it with your spouse. If your relationship currently is frosty, wait for a slight thaw. You don't need all-out warmth, but too icy an atmosphere is not a good venue for introducing a curious new idea.

Be alone with your spouse and not rushed. Don't try to squeeze minutes between the evening's dishes and the kids' soccer practice. And for sure, don't approach him when he's got the remote in his hand.

One prime time is in bed at night, assuming you still are in the same bed. If not, any private place will do. If your kids are wandering about, don't allow them to intrude or interrupt. Their "needs" can wait for an hour or so. If you're feeling self-conscious over what you're about to say, lower the lights. Something about dim lights and shadows creates a sense of anonymity, making your revelations flow more easily.

Use your list as a foundation, similar to the rough draft of a book. The outline is there, just not in fleshed-out form. Lest you're thinking, "It was all I could do to come up with these, and I'm supposed to elaborate? Can I interview anybody else—our kids, his mother, his second-grade teacher, his therapist, a judge?" That won't be necessary. A new direction in thinking is its own stimulus. Each thought fosters others in a branching fashion, leading to attributes you've ignored, denied, or just plain forgotten.

Do you revisit your list? That's your judgment call. You don't need to dust it off every few weeks, corner your spouse, and reiterate all his high points. Actors read scripts. Once committed to mind, the written list is no longer needed. Your list is a kind of guide. At any time and for any reason, you can add something and then unveil the "new, revised" version. Be slow to subtract items. That would sort of defeat the purpose.

Most beginning exercisers could benefit from a trainer. So here are a few list-sculpting pointers.

1. Be specific. Instead of, "You're thoughtful," or the backhanded, "You're thoughtful on occasion," try, "You always ask me how my day went." Rather than, "You have fun with the kids," point out, "They love how you tease them."

2. Specificity affords two main benefits. One, it makes the praise more tangible. It says, "I notice the particulars, the snippets of you." Two, it allows other details. "You're thoughtful" can encompass anything from "I can count on your remembering my birthday" to "You always put at least one of your socks in the clothes basket." Once used, "You're thoughtful" absorbs a whole range of possibilities that would mean more if identified individually. If my wife tells me, "You're cute," I'm curious

to know exactly how. Is it my winsome boyish charm or my muscular forearms? ("You're humble" probably wouldn't make the list.)

3. Stay positive. "You don't smell like a swamp after working outside" may be true, but there are likely countless other things he also doesn't smell like. "You didn't ignore my obnoxious relatives this holiday as much as you did last" wouldn't make anyone's Christmas list. Don't frame remarks in the "You're not as bad as you used to be" genre. Defensiveness could erupt before you get past compliment number two. Of course, you could then observe, "We made it farther than I thought we would."

4. Emphasize personality and character. "You've got great legs," to be sure, is nice to hear. But "You always work hard to keep yourself in shape" or "You have such a nice way of showing an interest in people" might be nicer to hear.

5. To a guy, "You have muscular arms" may not be as prized as "You're willing to watch movies I like even though I know that's not what you like."

Sometimes—I'll admit, more often earlier in our marriage, with fewer kids—my wife and I practiced a variant of "Make a List." Lying in bed at night, I might offer, "Let me tell you some things I like about you..." whereupon Randi would patiently listen to my twenty-minute monologue. After which I would hand her the list I had composed about myself and ask her just to sign it.

Resistance Rationale #1: "I can't think of much to say."
Aw, come on.

How's that for a highly trained professional's answer? Blame it on years of trying to understand my kids.

Why do kids so often answer, "I don't know," when asked

something? Are they so far removed from their own motives? Or are they really saying, "I haven't bothered to think about it"? If you're asking me, I'd say mostly the latter.

"Make a List" can meet the same response. It's not so much that we can't find good things to say; it's that we might not have thought much about it. Everyone has positives, even if those positives start with, "He waxes a car beautifully," or, "She makes the best potato soup." If you struggle to see your spouse's better sides, could that not be as much or more from your lack of practice rather than from his lack of attributes?

Then too, the clock is not giving you one hour to conjure up ten entries. Your spouse isn't even aware of your writer's block. Go slow. Take a mind-clearing nap. The longer you ponder, the better. More will come to mind with time.

Sometimes you might have to engage in a little psychological archeology, excavating qualities long buried under layers of emotions and history. While your husband may not spend all the time with the kids he once did, what time he now spends is good time. The years have found your father harder to please; still, your wife does try to reach out. Don't reject the good because it's not as good as it once was. Some of it is lingering, though weaker or more sporadic.

In a troubled marriage a spouse's once attractive qualities can go dormant. *Dormant* does not mean "dead." Those qualities can and do return often, more often if they're coaxed.

Break your list down. Start with those facets more objective than subjective: physical, occupational, talents, hobbies. They are more neutral and easier to concede. Next, consider your spouse's conduct toward others. While she may not always laugh with you, your wife might attract others with her sense of humor.

For most partners the toughest challenge comes with sorting through the bad and the ugly to find the good. Consistently appealing habits are no stretch to discern and appreciate. But most traits are a mix of highs and lows. What parts of your spouse's personality have merit within their imperfections? Is he not affectionate overall? Where and how is he still affectionate? Is she not the most communicative? What does she share? Is he a weak disciplinarian? When did he last stand his ground with the kids?

I am not as consistent or vigilant in day-to-day discipline as is my wife. Nonetheless she does lean upon my "Dad presence" for added backing. She is not the neatnik I am. Still, she resembles me more in that dimension now than twenty-five years ago.

A fascinating study asked partners to write down their spouse's weaknesses. I suspect a time limit had to be enforced. Each partner knew, in revealing detail, all in the other that screamed for fixing.

Next the researchers instructed, "Write down your own short-comings." Spouses needed much less time. What's more, the self-assessments were tempered by self-tolerance. "Sometimes I could be more pleasant," or "I could do a better job at keeping the house picked up." The study confirmed the expected: We are far more attuned to another's failings than to our own.

Framed differently, we tend to see ourselves more favorably than do others. Chances are your spouse credits to himself more positives and less negatives than you do. Of course, the converse is also probably true. You see yourself as more winsome than he does. Are you both totally self-deluded? Are you both myopic to what you're really like?

Could at least part of your self-perceptions be accurate? No doubt you'd like to believe so. Can you give your spouse the same benefit of the doubt? Could looking at him through his eyes—even having to squint to focus—offer some insight into his better qualities? Do you not see some of what he sees in himself because it's not there or because you'd rather not see it?

A few final questions: What originally attracted you to your spouse? What did you then admire about her? Are all those qualities gone, every last vestige of them?

Look back for list grist. Remnants of once-upon-a-time attributes can provide a push for a list stretching into the present.

Resistance Rationale #2: "She'll think she's easier to live with than she is."

One resistance rationale of "Say, 'I'm sorry'" argued, "My apology will lead her to believe I'm confessing when I'm not, that she's all right and I'm all wrong." The answer was that you are only accepting your own portion of blame, whether 1 percent or 100 percent. You are not implying anything more. Time will confirm that.

That Resistance Rationale and this one are relatives. "She'll think she's Mrs. Wonderful, with few if any faults." What if she *is* Mrs. Wonderful? (Is that her maiden name, or did she take yours at marriage?) Count your blessings, and skip past this section. Always let her know how glad you are she is.

If she's not Mrs. Wonderful, take a lesson from the previously cited marriage study, and look for a few wonderful aspects to her person. She likely has more than you think.

Many if not most spouses in marriage counseling want to get the other person psychologically fixed. "She needs to see what she's really like, so she can change." And I, as therapist, am to convince her of that. Sure, she needs self-scrutiny, but much of the time, she's not the only one.

If I were to start off spotlighting the marriage's strengths, some might wonder, "When do we begin the real therapy?" or, "From what matchbook cover did you send for your degree?" Their foremost goal is to identify for their spouse, with my input, the faulty stuff and correct it. Any focus on positives can wait or, in the extreme, is irrelevant.

Good therapy and good marriages are not either/or endeavors. That is, *either* we tackle the bad, *or* we uplift the good. Rather, they are both/and. We *both* tackle the bad *and* recognize the good. Even if you recite your list every Sunday, the rest of the week you live the marriage facts of life—the agreeable and the not so. About the only way your list could convince your spouse she's a saint is if, during all other times, you treat her as one. Makes sharing the list sound a lot easier now, doesn't it?

What if your wife does think, "It's about time you notice me for what I am"? It is true, you are noticing her for what she is. What else she is—which didn't make your list—has likely been far more often noticed, out loud. Bluntly put, your spouse's impression that she is all OK in your mind will probably take some hits during the next disagreement.

An adage says that our conduct is not so much influenced by what others think of us as by what we think they think of us. If someone compliments your upbeat nature, will you be more or less moved to act upbeat around her? If another tells you, "I so admire your natural humility," how will you feel? Pretty proud, I'd say. And you'd work harder to come across humble around him and maybe even with obtuse others who aren't yet in tune with your overwhelming meekness. We tend to act in the direction others see us.

Use this for your marriage. Comment on your spouse's better sides, and you may nudge him toward living more consistently those sides. What do you have to risk, other than some ego massaging?

Resistance Rationale #3: "I don't feel he deserves it."

A marriage battered by ill will provokes this reaction. Distressing emotions—anger, frustration, sadness—carry force. They are felt hard, sometimes long after the event that provoked them. To the degree that their voice marks the relationship, it gains volume, drowning out whatever is nicer but quieter.

However, the question is not "Do I *feel* he deserves it?" The question is "*Does* he deserve it?"

To assert that someone doesn't deserve praise in effect says one of two things. One, little is praiseworthy about him. We'll talk about this one shortly. Two, his demeanor is so unpleasant or difficult that he merits no accolades when it is not. To warrant praise one has to earn it by consistently praiseworthy conduct.

This reasoning has a flaw. It implies that a person must first change for the better before getting any credit for changing for the better. Could not giving credit first lead someone to change in the direction you'd like? Rather than "I won't say anything positive until I see more effort to be positive," how about "I will find some good in the midst of all the bad, in hopes of inching toward a better relationship"?

But what if he truly doesn't deserve credit? As a psychologist for over thirty years, I have encountered many who have socially and emotionally obliterated their lives and others' lives. Their more obvious pathologies alone could fill a couple of files. Yet, given one hour, I could dig and find some things admirable perhaps, not because I'm such an affirming type but because no one is Lucifer. "He loves his grandmother." Everyone, no matter how ugly or unpleasant, has aspects that aren't so.

When someone says, "It's hard to give her praise," I am prompted to ask, "What in you makes it hard?" Pent-up resentment? Unresolved hurt? Betrayal? Self-preservation? Laziness? Why exactly the reluctance to noting the most benign of habits, such as, "You keep the garage neat"? Look inward to scan your own motives for resistance. While legitimate, they may be clouding your full view.

Suppose you survey a sample of your friends and relatives. Sure enough, they agree—you haven't influenced them too much, have you?—that for every one of your spouse's positives, they see four negatives. Even so, do the four nullify the one? Does the one cease to be because it contrasts with the big picture? If I am surly with your mother, slow to pick up after myself, forget your birthday, and obsessively flick the remote every eight seconds, do any or all of these negate the fact that I am affectionate with our son?

The two middle letters of *list* are *is*. A list is what good there *is*. It is one side of marital reality. And most of the time, recognizing all sides of reality is a good way to live.

Resistance Rationale #4: "He'll wonder what I'm up to."

Someone has said, "Everything is really about something else." Meaning, the motives underlying someone's behavior are seldom the obvious ones. What is apparent is routinely misleading.

A bit of over-psychologizing, I think. Sometimes something is not about anything else. It is exactly what it looks to be.

Putting to paper another's better qualities and sharing them is, it seems likely, not something you've ever done. You may have had complimentary conversations, in which one warm word prompted reciprocation prompted re-reciprocation. That's distinct from writing out the content of those conversations for future marital use.

Some months back I visited a florist to buy flowers for my wife. No birthday, Sweetest Day, Valentine's Day—just because. I can hear some lady readers applauding me, "Awwww, how sweet." To be fully self-disclosing, I hadn't done anything like that since our wedding rehearsal dinner. OK, not quite that long, but it had been a while.

The female florist point-blank asked, "What did you do?"

I said, "Today or yesterday?"

She explained that nearly every guy who orders flowers in between the standard holidays is making amends for some mis-understanding or wrong. A fragrant apology, so to speak.

All that may be true for the average Joe, I thought, but my wife and I had a trust solidified by years. When I presented her with the flowers, she smiled sweetly, thanked me, kissed me, waited a few seconds, and then asked, "Should I know something?" I answered, "Did you ever work as a florist?"

The lesson? If giving flowers isn't a typical gesture, then giving flowers is a gesture inviting question, unless it's clear the receiver smells no ulterior motive. As emphasized throughout this book, "never before" conduct, however relationship-healthy, is prone to misinterpretation. Another has to make that conduct fit within her prevailing scheme of understanding.

Consequently, while your list's intent may not be outrightly questioned or impugned, you could face a cautious reaction. Don't be quick to conclude, "Well, that wasn't what I expected. I won't put myself in that position again." Know that you do have a potent ally: human nature. Your spouse does want to believe that what you're sharing is true. Further, she wants to believe that you believe it too.

To convince your spouse further of your sincerity, reiterate. What you verbalized once, verbalize again. Not by echoing your list tomorrow but by applying it to daily life. If you wrote, "You always fix me coffee in the morning just the way I like it," so note with your coffee. If you said, "I am amazed at how you take some of my uncle's wild opinions in stride," comment on her graciousness next time Uncle Arty waxes forth. Your list can be a personal reminder to remind her when and why you do appreciate her. Don't lay it to rest beneath an attitude of "I told you once what I like about you. We don't need to belabor it."

One caution: High frustration can warp any list into an emotional cudgel. "Maybe I spoke too quickly about your thoughtfulness in calling me if you have a change in schedule." "I think I should remove 'respect' if this is how you talk to me when you get mad." Or to play really rough, "I'm realizing now how much of my list is fiction."

Such reversals convey, "My good opinions of you are fragile. They can crack at any time." Never let the list be a fluctuating commentary on your spouse's moment-to-moment likability. That will turn praise into insults. It will also badly tarnish your credibility. Future compliments, listed or spontaneous, will face a higher wall of skepticism.

Of course, the better your relationship, the better your reception. If positive words are not alien to your marriage, the exercise itself may be a first, but its foundational principle is not. Compliments, oral or written, are a real and automatic part of your communication.

Someone else once said, "Everything isn't always about something else. Sometimes what you hear is what you get."

Resistance Rationale #5: "It would feel forced."

It is in a sense. Would you, unprompted, approach your spouse with "Let's sit down. I've written down some really good stuff about you"? Probably not, unless you've just read something like "Listing Your Way to a Happier, Healthier Marital You."

What is not natural manifestly feels unnatural. It requires a deliberate, conscious effort. Much of what I do in my life goes counter to what my "authentic self" would prefer. I have to make myself do it. Nevertheless, some amount of self-compulsion is self-enhancing.

Since college I've been an inveterate weight lifter. I can probably count on one hand the number of days I've walked into the gym anticipating, "This is bliss, straining against the earth's gravitational pull until my muscles scream." I did have a few such rushes in my early twenties, when my body was still brimming with vinegar. Throughout the rest of my years though, I've pushed myself with a mental cost-benefit analysis. The cost is time and effort; the benefit is more strength and, I hope, a healthier body.

Try an experiment. Tell a friend about your list plan. Will you hear, "Oh, did you read that article in *Marriage Today* too? Wasn't it inspiring? I was thinking about doing the exact same thing." Or will you hear, "I don't know if I could do that. I'd have to sit and think about it." Likely she'd have questions. What is your purpose? Why now? Are you fighting? In short, this isn't anything anybody she knows has ever tried.

"This isn't me" can block you from pursuing something that has benefit to you as well as to another. Don't ask, "Is it forced?" Ask, "Is it good?" And you may not know the answer to that until you force yourself.

The List Scenario

Wife: Can we talk for a little bit?

Husband: About what?

Therapist: "Can we talk?" can be marriage code for, "We've got a problem," "You've got a problem," or, "I'm going to reiterate what I don't like about you." Thus a spouse may warily try to establish the subject before acquiescing to "talk."

Wife: It's not about anything bad or any problem. It's something I've never done before. It's about you, and I think you'll be pleased.

Husband: OK.

Therapist: By reassuring husband, "This isn't going to hurt," Wife is assuaging his reservations about what is coming.

Wife: I've been doing lots of thinking lately, and I realize that I don't let you know very often what I appreciate and admire about you. I've been lazy about that.

Therapist: Whatever motive might underlie Wife's lack of complimentary effort, she wisely avoids expressing it. That would just push the exchange back toward, "We've got a problem." By briefly providing a motive—laziness—she answers the unspoken, "Why are you doing this now?"

Wife: I've decided I need to write down the things in you I admire. This paper isn't my cheat sheet. It's not to make me say things I don't believe. It's to remind me what I do think. It's not everything, but it's a start.

Husband: OK.

Therapist: Hubby still is withholding judgment. Were he completely at ease, he probably would be more encouraging. "Thank you," "Sounds good," "Can you put them in alphabetical order?"

Note also that Wife didn't get specific about how long she worked on her list. Getting too detailed can help or hurt. "I did this last night," is a far nicer compliment than, "I've been working at this since our daughter was in first grade," (the daughter who is now married with three kids).

Wife: Even if we argue about something, it's never too long before you tell me, "I love you." You always kiss me good-bye when you leave the house, and if we're out somewhere, you hold my hand.

Therapist: People are most attuned to what means most to them. The affection expressions are uppermost for Wife.

Husband: That's because you always offer your hand to me. I like that too.

Therapist: The wall of wariness is crumbling with the building praise. Not unexpectedly, Husband wants to reciprocate. He's not thinking, "Keep the compliments coming. You've only begun to scratch the surface of my worth." Many spouses will begin to respond in kind at some point during the accolades.

Wife: Well, maybe sometime you can do a list for me. But right now I want to talk about you.

Therapist: Nice gesture by Wife. She refocuses the conversation back onto Husband, while leaving an opening for him to do something similar at another time. She could offer to help him compose his list, but that might be a bit presumptuous.

Husband: Where did you get this idea? I mean, don't get me wrong. I like it, but I never would have expected it.

Wife: Maybe that's part of my problem. Saying nice things shouldn't be so few and far between.

Therapist: Something tells me that if Hubby ever does detail his wife's better qualities, he'll have no shortage of material.

The Last Word

The inclination to praise contracts as apathy or ill will expands. Noticing a spouse's good points retreats in the face of more perceived bad points. To reverse the negative momentum takes a deliberate decision. It takes a recognition that it can be reversed and that it will be worth it.

To quote the ancient philosopher, "A journey of a thousand miles begins with a single step." Gathering good words together in one place—first in mind, then on paper—is that first small step. Telling your spouse its contents is the second step. It is, in the words of another source of philosophy—*Star Trek*—to boldly go where one hasn't gone before.

Start the journey, and you may find it leads to an unexplored marital world, one you would find a very hospitable place to inhabit.

| *Add a Touch* |

A common theme emerges in marital therapy: Affection is low at best, absent at worst. One partner, not always the female, craves it more than the other, though routinely the supply is short for both. In order to cope, many spouses learn to live with less. They've come to think that's just the way it is because that's just the way it's been, if not since the beginning then since the beginning of troubles.

Of course, lack of affection typically reflects the relationship's overall temperature. As the atmosphere cools, affection slips into hibernation. Then again, sometimes a marriage isn't all that cold. Affection, like compliments, chills from lack of effort.

Poll a hundred couples, and a majority, I anticipate, would prefer more physical warmth. I doubt anyone would complain, "There is way too much touching, hugging, and kissing between us. It's getting old. I think it's actually hurting our deeper emotional connection." No matter how much affection embraces our marriage, most of us would welcome more.

An unpopular rule of life states, if you want more of something, you may have to give more of it. A more unpopular rule of life states, changing oneself is easier than changing someone else. Blending these rules, if you're one who wants more touches, physical or emotional, you might have to reach out first.

A study of restaurant servers and customers came to an interesting finding. Servers who gently (and appropriately) touched customers received significantly higher tips.[1]

How did so tiny an act elicit such favor? After all, we can assume these were two or more strangers in an informal setting. Apparently some kind of social link occurred. Whether the server conveyed, "I see you as more than a faceless tip," or the customer sensed, "I'm a little more special than the average eater here," the fact is, the more touchy servers received more warmth, as measured in dollars and cents, than the less touchy.

Any kind of affection—a hug, a kiss, an arm around the waist, a holding of hands—to be sure, is a touch. Small step #10 is even more basic; it's affection at its most elemental level. Anytime, anywhere, at least once a day, touch your spouse in a gentle, sweet, or warm manner. Any physical contact—nothing negative, of course—that conveys, "I know you're here, and I want you to know that I know," is what matters.

If affection is at the heart of your marriage, and daily you average sixteen touches of every kind, this step is an afterthought for you. Still, can you add another touch, one you don't routinely do: rub of the neck, kiss of the hand, stroking of hair or arm? Find something different from your norm.

If your marriage watches days pass without the slightest physical gesture, the most minor move could be a major hurdle. It also has the most potential for good. Every fitness trainer knows that benefits accrue fastest to those who move from no exercising to some exercising, even if not all that intense. In a year their strength can double or triple. Those who are longtime exercisers do not see such dramatic gains. Still, they can maintain an impressive fitness level.

Humans have a built-in need for one-to-one contact. From birth every infant needs ample holding, rocking, and caressing for peak development. The innate drive for the physical never is outgrown, though we vary widely in how much we seek it, resist it, or learn to live without it.

Touch says many things: I love you; I'm sorry; I'm not angry; Thank you; What's on your mind? Nice job; I'm here for you; Hi; I like you with me; I'm listening; I understand; Please tell me; Are you all right? Can I play cards with the guys tonight? I was dealt a no on this last one, until I added a few more "touches," like vacuuming the family room and putting all the kids to bed myself.

Is this overinterpreting the meaning of a touch? Psychologists are prone to overinterpretation. We're also prone to answer a question with questions. How often have you felt a warm message from a silent touch? What was the message—comfort, acceptance, concern? Have you ever been at a loss for the right words but used touch to talk? How about to someone grieving? Have you ever used a nonverbal action to tone down the rancor of a verbal dispute?

Few things give more emotional bang for your buck than a touch. And you don't have to be a server to feel it.

Resistance Rationale #1: "I'm not an affectionate person."
You don't need to be. Smothering your mate with smooches isn't the goal. For some spouses that would be no small step; that would be a running leap across the Grand Canyon. Every step proposed in this book is meant to be within anyone's reach. Granted, some may be seldom taken, but none require personality reconstruction.

If by nature you're a quiet individual, do you never talk? If you're a couch athlete, are you incapable of running or tossing a ball? If you're shy, do you shy away from every social situation?

When someone says, "That's not who I am," most of the time he's actually saying, "That's not consistently who I am." Almost never does he mean, "Under no circumstances do I ever deviate from my normal pattern."

If you're not affectionate, do you never touch anyone? How about your mother? A little baby? Your pet cat? No doubt you shake hands. You may chest-bump a buddy during a sporting event. If a woman, maybe you've never high-fived your girlfriend, but most likely you exchange personal signs of friendship. Some touch is acceptable, initiated even, for nearly everyone under chosen circumstances.

Enveloping your spouse with a bear hug and twelve-second kiss may stretch you way beyond your physical bounds. Would a small peck on the cheek with your "Bye" be insurmountable? A hand on the shoulder, a guiding palm in the small of the back, an arm to help another out of a vehicle—any one of these can signal care or aid without being overtly affectionate.

Most parents seeking my discipline guidance are convinced they have a strong-willed child. Most do not. They have a child who is strong-willed with them. By "wiring" the child is no more strong-willed than most. By learning, however, he has become more contrary with his parents than with anybody else. "The teacher said she wished she had a whole room full of him. I thought I was at the wrong school."

Similarly, one who claims, "I'm just not all that affectionate," often means, "I'm just not all that affectionate with my spouse." By inclination she may well be more affectionate than she shows, but as the marriage has languished, her longing to touch or be touched has likewise languished. Though barely breathing, in reality it is still quite alive.

Ask yourself, "At one time did I touch more?" If yes, that raises another question: Which is you, then or now? If you were more expressive then, were you living counter to your personality? Or did you once genuinely feel more warm to the touch? If so the old you is the real you. Presently you may not be acting affectionate; that doesn't mean you're not an affectionate person.

Resistance Rationale #2: "My spouse isn't affectionate."

Do you mean, "He doesn't want affection"? Do you mean, "He doesn't like affection"? Do you mean, "He won't return affection"?

"He doesn't want affection" is different from "He doesn't want to be touched." As we've said, all physical affection is touch, but not all touch is physical affection. Touch, being more subtle, doesn't arouse the resistance that stronger affection might. In the main it is acceptable to even the most affection-resistant spouses.

Has your spouse always been so unaffectionate? Just as you might have once been more touch-inclined, was your spouse likewise? If so then his willingness, though now buried, may still be capable of resuscitation, even without mouth-to-mouth. His current lack of affection may be due more to your emotional than your physical relationship. You can't identify which until someone —guess who?—starts to reach out. A spouse's rejecting of something may be a defense rather than a sign of no desire.

"He doesn't like affection" would be a rare attitude. So hard-wired are we for touch that children who recoil from any sort of physical contact are often diagnosed with a developmental or neurological disorder. To dismiss the smallest token of affection, your spouse has to dismiss his biology. The circumstances he finds acceptable may be limited, but a, "No touch, please," runs counter to the collective and constant human proclivity.

"He doesn't like affection," and, "He doesn't want affection" are not the same assertion. One can like something and still not want it. I can absolutely crave a triple-thick blueberry malt but, for gastrointestinal reasons, not want it. Conversely, I can want to exercise, even religiously so, but not like it. The linguistic tendency is to hear both statements as interchangeable, when often they are quite dissimilar.

A spouse can desperately long for more contact but dismiss it for all manner of reasons—resentment, hurt, aloofness. Under better conditions she would be more receptive. It isn't that she doesn't want it; it's that for the meantime she doesn't like it, as it isn't consistent with where she sees the marriage.

Now on to, "He won't return affection." It's a good marriage in which everything taken together is relatively balanced. It's an uncommon marriage in which spouses are equally expressive, equally talkative, equally sacrificing, equally anything. To expect reciprocation to be the norm in each dimension of a relationship is to invite frustration.

My wife is far more thoughtful than I in giving the kids little notes in backpacks, candy on Valentine's Day, and unexpected dessert treats. I, on the other hand, impart the weightier guidance for a lifetime: "Don't punch your brother when he isn't looking." We're not alike in lots of ways, but we are a team.

Your mate may not return an eye for an eye or a touch for a touch. Still, that isn't the sole measure of whether or not you're making yourself felt. "I'm five times more touching than he is, and I always have been. I'd be content with even a four-to-one ratio." Yes, but your five-to-one isn't solely physical. It's an emotional glue holding you together more tightly. Because another doesn't respond in like manner doesn't necessarily mean that he doesn't want what you offer, doesn't appreciate it, or wouldn't severely miss it if absent.

Have you ever watched soft rain pelting sunbaked ground? The first billion or so drops, if countable, have little noticeable impact. The ground seems as stubborn as ever. But sometime during that watering—who can possibly discern when?—the turf softens, becoming muddy even and ready for seed.

The analogy isn't perfect. Your touches don't need to tally billions, and likely your spouse is not that arid. Nevertheless your little drops of affection will soak into his surface. And how he'll respond remains to be felt, if not in a physical return then in other seemingly unrelated pieces of thoughtfulness.

The story goes that a member of a church's congregation writes his pastor a public letter criticizing his bland sermons. His complaint is "I've listened for ten years, and I'm hard-pressed to remember anything specific about them."

Another member of the congregation, moved to respond, writes, "After thirty years of marriage, I would be hard-pressed to recall the exact contents of any meal my wife has prepared for me. Nevertheless, taken all together, those meals were a lifetime of pleasure and, more than that, kept me alive."

So it is with touch. The specifics—the when, where, how, how much—may not be all that memorable. It is the cumulative effect that nurtures, sustains, softens.

Resistance Rationale #3: "He won't even notice."
Notice that I used the masculine pronoun, *he*, here. That is delib-

erate. Women notice. As a gender they are more socially aware than men. In my marriage my wife notices everything about me, at all times, forever. If I observe a change in her hairstyle, I get extra credit.

I have five sons and five daughters. At the end of my oldest daughter, Hannah's, first day of kindergarten, she could recite her teacher's full name—married and maiden—favorite television shows as a child, favorite songs (with words), social security number, as well as her daughters' middle names and favorite colors (puce, magenta, and ecru). My oldest son, Andrew, was fuzzily aware that he went to a class of some sort, run by a lady whose name was "teacher" and who had them do "stuff."

Now, this is not to excuse anyone's obliviousness. It is to accept reality. As a group women are far more likely to notice the slightest change, particularly one for the better. Getting a husband to notice might take a few more repetitions. "Andrew, what is your teacher's last name?" "I don't think she told anybody, Dad. I'll find out by Christmas."

What does it mean to notice? Does it mean that one can pinpoint, "Hey, I've been counting, and you've touched me sweetly nine times this week"? Or does it mean to be aware that something in some way is changing?

Intuition is a priceless gift. It is a sharpened sense, initially below the level of words, of a situation's meaning. It is evidenced by the police officer whose instincts are on high alert though no signs of danger are yet obvious; the mother who just knows, when no one else has an inkling, that something is bothering her taciturn son; the therapist who hears the core issue before it is verbalized. Intuition is the brain's marvelous ability to absorb and digest a huge amount of incoming data and reach a conclusion based on past experience. All the while the person's not able to explain exactly how the brain "knew."

Your spouse may not immediately realize what it is that's warmer about you, but he may feel it. As the feeling progresses, so too will his ability to identify its cause.

Defeated parents regularly tell me that their child doesn't seem to care if he's disciplined. If they send him to the corner thirty-six times, his attitude each time is "So what? I like it here." Little Spike is just good at making the best of a bad scene.

My advice? Continue the corner. With visits 37 through 103, a shift in reaction does occur. The once tolerable vertex morphs into a discipline drag. Visits 104 through infinity effect a turnabout. Spike starts to behave better.

Added touches 1 through 36 may not register on a spouse's radar. Or if they do, they may be interpreted as momentary blips, random happenings. Touches 37 through 103 signal that some shift is occurring, though why and for how long remains cloudy. Touches 104 and beyond clear up the message, even for the most obtuse husband, who in fact may not be as obtuse as he appears. Isn't this the same guy who is acutely cognizant of the time—to the day, hour, and minute—that his favorite football team foolishly called a draw play on third down and twelve? All of us notice what we're primed to notice, what we consider important.

Resistance Rationale #4: "I'm already showing most of the affection."

Let me begin with a compliment. It's impressive that you continue to reach out in the face of minimal or near zero return. No doubt you have done much for your relationship. Had you not so persevered, where would your marriage otherwise be?

For many years I was a consultant to special education teachers who taught SBH, or "severe behavior handicapped," classes. They worked with the kids whose classroom conduct was too disruptive for a regular educational setting. Toward the end of the school year, a teacher could wrestle with discouragement, telling me, "I'm not sure I've done anything positive for this child. He hasn't changed much since September."

To which I'd reply, "Well, that makes you one of the best teachers he's had. Before he came to you, he had been heading downhill for years. With you, his descent stopped. You leveled him out. At least now time might work with us instead of against us."

Giving all or most of the affection might seem to evoke little but an "I don't care if you do or don't" demeanor. Even so, you can't always realize the salutary effects of your actions unless you stop doing them, which I wouldn't advise. That would be a costly experiment.

If you're convinced that you're already living at peak affection, bypass this step. How's that again? A self-help author advising to ignore what he advises? Well, if you're already doing what I advise, you're a step ahead of me.

I do have other advice though. One, ask yourself, "What does touch do for me?" Conscious moves to make a warm marriage warmer or a cool one less cool are not without their own reward. Perhaps, "Touching makes me feel closer." Or, "My affection does bring out his nicer side." Or, "At least I have the satisfaction of saying I'm giving it my all." It's hard to try hard and not gain something of personal benefit.

Two, expand your repertoire. Most of us have a profile of preferred touch. Some are huggers; some are neck massagers; some are hand holders; some are foot warmers. Reach for a touch not among your standards. It will stand out.

Three, ask your spouse about your physical language. Get the specifics—what she notices, finds comforting, most appreciates. Sometimes someone won't say what she thinks until you directly ask her what she thinks. You might be surprised to find that your affection is doing more than you thought.

Social psychologists talk about a person's "love language"— meaning everyone has his own personal style for sending and receiving love. One spouse's preferred communication, verbal and otherwise, may not be his partner's. Knowing your spouse's most naturally received love message can add meaning to any gesture.

Action is my preferred love language. I may think that by painting the closet I tell my wife how much I care. I did give it two coats. She might want me to hold her in the morning, mingle in a few caresses, and then paint the closet.

Touching Scenario

Wife: Can I ask you something?

Husband: Sure.

Wife: You seem kind of different lately. I don't know exactly what it is, but you seem nicer to me. Is it my imagination?

Husband: What do you mean?

Therapist: Whether Hubby knows it or not, he's employing a common counselor tactic. Seek clarification when confronted by a question you're not sure how to answer.

A subtle increase in affection can cause the effect before the cause is identified. Wife feels something good is occurring. Just exactly what she can't identify.

Wife: You're not as preoccupied or distant. You seem more approachable.

Therapist: Interesting irony. Wife says Husband is more approachable. In fact, he is the one doing the approaching. She interprets his reaching out as an invitation to her to reach out. Touch shortens distance from both directions.

Husband: Well, I've been trying a little harder to treat you better. I think you deserve it.

Wife: Whatever it is, don't take this wrong, but it's a nice change.

Husband: I'm going to try to keep it up, but you know me. Sometimes I start out good and then slip.

Therapist: A little genuine self-insight improves another's tolerance for one's foibles. Not a false humility but an honest acknowledgment of one's weaknesses. It can work relational wonders.

Wife: I don't know what I'm doing differently to make you seem different. I can't figure it out, but I like it.

Husband: Well, I like it too. And I'm going to try to keep it up.

Therapist: For whatever reason, Husband is dodging the specifics of what he is doing differently. He may think if he confesses, "I'm touching you more," Wife may think, "It can't be that simple." He may want his new habit to gain a little more staying power. Or he could offer a generic, "I'm trying to be more affectionate in little ways." In time he might reveal what those ways are, or more likely, his wife will figure it out.

The Last Word

The word *touch* infuses our language: "That song touches my heart." "Your presence here touches me." "I'm too touched for words." "I'm a soft touch." The word itself reaches toward something deep in us, a built-in need to connect.

A touch can be the slightest of gestures, sometimes uncon-scious, often seemingly insignificant. In the world of gestures, a touch is a whisper, but its voice is unmistakable. Far beyond any effort they require, touches build upon one another to create the impression, "You matter." With touch the whole is much larger than the parts.

"I Don't Want To"

Very early in this book I observed that anything can be a justification for something you really don't want to do. Each Resistance Rationale for each small step toward a better marriage has the potential to be driven by a deeper resistance: *I don't want to.*

For the most skilled therapists, it's often not easy to uncover what someone's real resistance is. Is it the one admitted, or is the one admitted a substitute for the core resistance, that is, "I'm just not of the mind, or feeling, to"? What's more, questioning one's own motives does not come naturally. However convinced I am, for example, that my apology will be rejected, misheard, or misunderstood, closer internal scrutiny might reveal something more basic underlying my objections.

The reasoning can be circular. "I'm not about to apologize." Why not? "Because it won't be accepted." How do you know? "Other apologies weren't." Why don't you try? This time might be different. "Maybe, but I don't want to risk it." Why not? "Because it won't be accepted."

Whatever the resistance, the real-life effect is the same: behavioral paralysis. Ironically, *I don't want to* bars one from doing the very things that would make his marriage, and his life, more like he'd want.

No doubt you've had someone seek your guidance for a troubling situation. Upon advising you hear a string of objections: That won't work; I've tried that; it's not possible; he wouldn't listen. After a while, doesn't it get hard to stifle the urge to shout, "Then why did you ask me?"

The earliest psychotherapists put a name to this phenomenon. They called it *resistance*. In therapy language resistance is a person's defense against the therapist's observations and guidance—his emotional push back, if you will.

But why would someone seeking help, from a professional no less, resist the very help he seeks? My in-depth, therapeutic analysis? Because he doesn't want it.

Oh, he does want some sort of help. He's just not sure what kind or how much. The cost in effort or the cost to his self might be too high. Do the solutions involve making the first move, changing too much in himself, or striving to understand someone he presently doesn't like much? In short, maybe he wants things to change, but he doesn't want to change.

Sometimes the easier part of doing therapy is knowing what will work. The harder part is persuading someone to do it. *I don't want to* lies at the heart of the human condition. It is ingrained in who we are.

Fortunately, it's not so deeply entrenched that we can't overcome it. We do have it within ourselves to resist our own resistance. We just have to want to.

So here are a few pointers:

1. Accept the reality that what you think are your reasons may not be your reasons. Recognize that other motives are possible and may be beyond your immediate awareness.

2. Look deeper and longer within. Do some self-therapy. If all my objections could be answered, would I still be reluctant to act? If I were to be totally reassured that nothing I fear will actually happen, would that make a difference? Put another way, if every bit of my resistance were dispelled to my satisfaction, would I still be resistant? Searching for answers will help reveal how much *I don't want to* is at the bottom of my reasoning, constraining my better instincts.

3. Don't confuse *I don't want to* with *I don't feel like it.* They're not always synonymous. Feelings are transitory. What you might not feel inclined toward today, you could next week or even in one hour.

4. Feelings, particularly negative ones, are not consistent guides to action. They can impel you toward conduct you know is not right and away from that which is. Don't allow emotions to be the primary drivers of your behavior. They are far too fickle.

The final point is the most critical: Once you realize that *I don't want to* could be part of your resistance, tell yourself, "So what?" Meaning, whether or not you want to is a meaningless question. It is irrelevant. The only questions to ask are "Is this good? Is this what I should do for myself and my spouse?"

Doing what you don't want to do, because it's a good thing to do, will lead you toward what you wanted to do all along: make a better marriage.

The Ladder

As my ninth-grade Latin teacher used to reiterate, "Repetition for emphasis." In learning a second language, the more one hears the new vocabulary, the sooner the language becomes second nature.

With my Latin teacher's words still reverberating in my memory, I emphasize one more time my small steps to big marriage rewards. Together they form a ladder to a higher level of marital satisfaction.

Small Step #1: Say, "I'm Sorry"

If not in the top two most healing words, *I'm sorry* has to be in the top ten. It's a major psychological paradox that words brimming with so much good for all involved can be such a struggle to say out loud. One needn't be 100 percent in the wrong to be moved to say them. Any little parcel of blame can be cause for a heartfelt "I'm sorry."

Be the first to express regret, and doing so will get easier, not merely from practice but from receiving the reaction and reciprocation likely to come from your spouse.

Even those of us most faultless—in our own eyes—have a hefty capacity to say the hurtful, do the harmful, entertain the hostile. Morally maturing is the work of a lifetime. The transformation begins with the recognition of when you've done wrong and when to *say you're sorry*.

Small Step #2: Don't Say It

For better or worse, none of us is Mr. Spock, the alien character on the old television series *Star Trek*, who determined to act only by reason. Even Spock never succeeded in eliminating every vestige of emotion. It lived still, deep in his personality.

We will never conquer all hurtful emotions. Emotions are part of who we are. But we are endowed also with a will, the intellectual, decision-making part of us, to rein in any bad effects of those emotions. And one of the worst is the words that accompany them.

Practice silence for seconds during the peak surge of emotion, and the urge to put that emotion into words will recede. Better judgment will be allowed critical moments to assert itself, if not every time then enough of the time to avoid much relational damage. Follow this rule: When you feel most pressured to say it, *don't say it.*

Small Step #3: Listen a Minute

You don't learn much by talking. And if you want to know what another thinks and feels, especially about you, you learn nothing by talking. You must listen. Not only will you learn but also you'll soothe. Staying quiet and attentive, however briefly, puts a brake on an escalating cycle of words and emotions.

Give your spouse one uninterrupted minute. You'll receive a clearer picture of how she sees you and your marriage. You'll also quiet her mood. It's hard to feel unrelentingly upset toward someone who is giving you both ears. And when you do speak, you'll know better of what you speak if you *listen a minute.*

Small Step #4: Ask a Few Questions

Socrates taught his students by asking them questions. He probed for what they thought, how they thought, and why they thought it. Whether married or not, he had a wisdom about relationships. He understood that people want to be understood, especially by those close to them, like their philosophy teacher or spouse.

Listening and questioning are a synergistic tandem. They accommodate one another. Listening encourages freer expression. And freer expression encourages questions. It is said, "You can't know unless you ask." Or more to the point, you can't know someone's mind and heart unless you ask. Listening is the first step to understanding, but to understand more and better, you have to *ask a few questions.*

Small Step #5: Accept It

One aim of any kind of counseling, personal or professional, is to change behavior and its accompanying attitudes. Listening starts the process; questioning continues it. Why is another thinking, feeling, and acting so? Answers come from the willingness not only to hear what is being said but also, at some level, to accept it. Only then can there be progress.

Disagreements in marriage, especially intense verbal ones, can be lessened by an honest effort to accept, for the moment, the other's position or reasoning. You may be dumbstruck by what you hear. You may consider it downright ridiculous. You may not understand in the least how anyone could see it so. Nevertheless, to tone down the rancor and to nudge your spouse to look more closely at himself, just for a little while, *accept it.*

Small Step #6: Dump the D Word

Words can move a marriage in any direction. They can build or destroy. One of the more if not most destructive words to assault a marriage is the *D* word—*divorce.* Its utterance alone, even if lacking intent, can foster disillusion, detachment, or depression. It invites the thought of the formerly unthinkable.

At first sound the *D* word may be a probing for reaction or a threat to prod a partner toward a little more cooperation. Once introduced into the marital discourse, however, divorce can evolve from the possible to the probable to the preferred.

Divorce is a door most spouses would hope to leave closed. If at all possible, stay away from that door. *Dump the* D *word.*

Small Step #7: Use Your Manners

Familiarity breeds contempt. So goes the old and harsh saying. More precisely, it seems, familiarity breeds laziness. And few dimensions of familiarity are as prone to laziness as the use of good words. And few good words decay more quickly than the simplest: manners.

More than socially conditioned exercises in etiquette, manners carry a broader message: "I respect you. You are worth my affording you the same courtesy I afford to others, often conscientiously so. Indeed, you deserve more."

Manners speak their meaning through repetition. Polite words add worth and a pleasing sound to any words they precede or follow. Draw a grown-up lesson from those little preschool unmarrieds: *Use your manners.*

Small Step #8: Protect

There is only one foolproof way to escape discipline disagreements between spouses: Don't let the children in the house, at least not when you're awake. While father and mother often discipline differently, the ideal is that each complements what the other lacks.

Seldom anymore are men called to protect women from threats like cougars and bears. Nowadays the perils are closer to home and, some would say, more menacing: the kids. Men, use your God-given male attributes to protect your wife from childish disrespect and mistreatment. She will appreciate it more than you realize, and the benefits to your parenting will extend well into your marriage.

Women, allow your husband to be a strong disciplinarian, in the finest sense of the words. For men the instinct is hard-wired, the instinct to *protect*.

Small Step #9: Make a List

Do you know what your spouse likes about you? I mean, really likes, down to the bits and pieces? Does your spouse really know what you like about her? Do you know? Could you write it down?

More telling, would you find it harder to list the positives than the negatives? The most solid marriages can atrophy in their acknowledgment of the other's attributes. In those most strained, the criticisms can bury the compliments.

Recall what you once admired about your spouse. Some of it must still be there, in some measure. Ponder her present attributes—physical, emotional, moral. Whatever the bad, it doesn't invalidate the good. Work your memory, massage your perceptions, uncover the positives. You may find a picture that you've long ignored or denied. Take the picture from mind to paper. Share it with your spouse.

One quick way to restore some balance to the words in a relationship is to *make a list*.

Small Step #10: Add a Touch

Savvy counselors listen to the words of language. Savvier counselors listen also to the words of the body or, body language. What is another saying when he is not talking? Sometimes a whole lot.

Speaking well to your spouse may involve no words at all but gestures. The simplest yet often most profound words of the body's language come through touch. Requiring little in the way of effort, a touch conveys much in the way of marital expression —love, acceptance, admiration, concern.

If you want to speak warmly and you can't always find the right words, *add a touch.*

N o t e s

Introduction

1. See Linda Waite and Maggie Gallagher, *The Case for Marriage: Why Married People Are Happier, Healthier, and Better Off Financially* (New York: Broadway, 2001), p. 148.

Small Step #6: Dump the *D* Word

1. See Waite and Gallagher, p. 70.

Small Step #10: Add a Touch

1. Franklin Crawford, "Researcher in consumer behavior looks at attitudes of gratitude that affect gratuities," www.news. cornell.edu.

About the Author

Dr. Ray Guarendi is the father of ten, clinical psychologist, author, public speaker, and nationally syndicated radio host. His radio show, *The Doctor Is In*, can be heard weekdays on Ave Maria Radio, EWTN, and SiriusXM. Dr. Ray also hosts his own national television show, *Living Right With Dr. Ray*. He has been a regular guest on national radio and television, including *Oprah, The 700 Club*, and *CBS This Morning*. His first book, *You're a Better Parent Than You Think!*, is now in its twenty-eighth printing. Other books include *Discipline That Lasts a Lifetime; Good Discipline, Great Teens; Adoption: Choosing It, Living It, Loving It*; and *Winning the Discipline Debates: Dr. Ray Coaches Parents*.